The Elder: Minister of Mission

Edited by Paul M. Edwards

2

The Elder:
Minister of Mission

Edited by Paul M. Edwards

Library of Congress Cataloging-in-Publication Data
The elder: minister of mission / edited by Paul M. Edwards.

    p. cm.

Includes bibliographical references and index.

ISBN 0-8309-0770-X

1. Elders (Church officers) 2. Reorganized Church of Jesus Christ of Latter Day Saints—Doctrines. I. Edwards, Paul M.

BX8675.E43 1997

262'.149333—dc21   97-7398

CIP

Contents

Preface

As with any writing project, many individuals were involved in creating this one. Of prime significance are the authors who have shared not only their insights but also their talents. Mark Scherer, RLDS World Church historian, has focused his specialty on the office of elder, bringing us historical insights. Wayne Ham, administrator of the Master of Arts in Religion at Temple School Center, gives us a significant look at the scriptural foundations of priesthood. Darlene Caswell, curriculum coordinator for Temple School Center, has placed the role of the elder in community.

Looking at the diverse and complex role of the elder, several authors have addressed specific themes. Larry McGuire, World Church appointee from Chicago; Joni Wilson and Paul M. Edwards of Temple School Center; and Barbara L. Carter, World Church appointee from Springfield, Missouri, have each addressed an aspect of the elder's mission, holding up their thoughts for your consideration.

Jerry Nieft, World Church appointee at Far West Stake; Shelby M. Barnes, a historian from Alabama; Ruth Ann Wood, coordinator of the editorial office at Temple School Center; Jeanne Earnest, a psychologist in private practice in Missouri, have looked at the role of the elder in light of the church focus on vision, mission, and celebration.

The production of this work also has depended on the help of the Temple School Center staff, especially the continued assistance of Beverly Spring; the research validation of Joni Wilson; the help of Ruth Ann Wood's high standards of copy editing; the professional skills of Charlotte Faris in providing the final manuscript; and on Tammy Lindle, Linda Wagner, Francie Dickensheets, and Rhonda Melling for keeping the wolves at bay.

The hope of those who contributed to this volume is that it will help in the formation of your priesthood contribution, as well as your personal growth toward your Creator.

Introduction

Paul M. Edwards

This book addresses the role of the elder, specifically those serving in this priesthood capacity within the community and congregation. Never has the influence of this office been more desperately needed, nor has the value of the elder's contribution been more readily identified. Thus, this book emerges out of the great respect held for those men and women who, called to this significant role, have accepted the responsibility related to it and who are living their lives in the acceptance of mission. For that is the calling: the call to mission.

The term we use, elder, comes to us from the Hebrew word *zaqen* which at first identified the person, and the responsibility, of the oldest son. Later the concept was pluralized to mean a collection of older sons, usually referring to some form of their legislative or judicial responsibilities. It reflected what their culture suggested were the best minds of the society.

A second use of the word is in reference to a person's age. Age, in traditional terms, meant the characteristics of that advanced age: wisdom and experience. Under the Mosaic regime, the tribal elders formed an advisory body or council that assumed the wisdom of its members. The council, therefore, was constituted and called into action to deal with those issues within the society that required wisdom in their consideration. In the current societies of the Western world, the term usually implies age without suggesting wisdom.

Within the Restoration movement, however, the term defines those members of the priesthood who, though not selected by age or gender, reflect experience, wisdom, and a special regard for things spiritual. It is a term suggesting a call peculiar to the needs of the congregation.

The responsibilities of the elder, in the main, balance between the dual responsibilities as pastor and presider. For it is primarily the elder who must shoulder the burden, as well as taste the joys, of congregational leadership, and thus to carry the needs of the people and the concerns of the community. These roles together ask of the elder the willingness to represent the love of Jesus Christ while being God's people to the world.

When we look at ourselves today, we, like most every generation, tend to believe that our time is vastly different from all other times. To a large measure, we believe that our time is vastly superior; the great strides and successes overshadow the increased failure and isolation. In all honesty, it is perhaps more true of this generation than most.

But history has recorded several significant periods through which civilized people have moved during which there have been fundamental shifts in the values of the time. These periods are so significant in the understanding of ourselves that we usually name them and base our memories on the period of change.

There was the great "beginning" that we call the Hellenistic period, then the Middle Ages, and so forth. Each period reflected the alterations, the blending of cultures, the division of intellectual and spiritual trends, and eventually the formation of accepted pluralism. This, of course, eventually became the accepted reality against which the future generation would need to rebel.

Today's world, often defined as postmodern, is but the current example of the flow and ebb of these world trends. I suggest it is no greater than any of the others but indeed a significant period that is forming around instant knowledge (not wisdom), transworld communication, and the integration of culture and commercialism (for example, Russians tearing down the great wall to get to the McDonald's walk-through).

What is lacking in this current cultural transformation now gaining strength is an identification of the center; that is, what are the foundations that hold us to the task? For while it is now possible to focus our skybound cameras on the inner expectations of every human, it is also true that the interrelationships of people are weak and that we suffer from a failure to address the intrinsic community-character resident in us all. The great unity promised by communication dissolves before the onslaught of identified diversity.

This concern lies no less on the people of the Restoration than on any other segment of the world. It lies more heavily perhaps because we have responded to the call to human purpose and strive toward a community of souls under the leadership of the Lord of creation. Unless we identify, and preserve, the inner core that holds us together, we shall become proponents of pluralism rather than defenders of diversity.

Modern religion—and this is certainly true of the Restoration movement—appears to maintain that the response to our great new knowledge, communication, and diversity lies in identifying some meaning to life. Such meaning comes as a goal, and the goal is formed in faith that a better system or greater organization or more attractive model can aid us in our meeting with life.

Yet, for religion, like so many human activities, it is not so much the meaning of life and meaning in life that is significant. A major contribution the church can make is to aid people in preserving the strength for living. Certainly that strength arises from the core of our beliefs—the nature of our God and the promise of Jesus Christ—and it is to the presentation and application of these beliefs that we are called.

Torn as many of us are between the demands on our time and the beliefs of our souls, we appear paradoxically unaware of our essential natures. Prone to sophistication and the complexity of questions, we are at the same time inclined to provide simplistic answers. As Vaclav Havel suggested: "By day, we work with statistics; in the evening, we consult astrologers and frighten ourselves with thrillers about vampires."*

The problem we face in this time is how it is that we might find the key to global multiculturalism. How can we identify some method or system that upholds individual human need and the rights of personal freedom, but that is anchored in a meaningful core that provides us the power and security of foundations to be different?

Sometimes the difficulty we have in dealing with our religious journey is that it begins in fear or anger or frustration rather than in joy and celebration. This should not be too hard for many to understand. We realize many people are driven nearly to despair by life's struggles before they are willing to open themselves to the soothing voice potential with God. By this time, they have become angry and afraid.

The answer, or at least some significant part of the answer, lies in the character of our beliefs. For what we seek and what we need seem to be much the same: we are in need of harmony among ourselves and our environment, our time and space, our friends and the community of humans, and God and community. We are all different but we are, as well, linked in some awesome way with all the others of this world and cosmos.

The call to mission is a call to share with God the burden of a world in distress. It is a worthy call for a willing people. We invite you to consider with us some aspects of this priesthood ministry.

---

* Vaclav Havel, president of the Czech Republic, speech given at Independence Hall, Philadelphia (July 4, 1994), "The Need for Transcendence in the Postmodern World," tearsheet in possession of the author.

Chapter 1

Melchisedec Ministry: Scripture, History, Congregation

Darlene Caswell, Wayne Ham, and Mark Scherer

In Scripture

Our Christian faith affirms with assurance that Christ has been present to the world in all epochs of history. Most important for us, Christ is revealed in our times and to our societies. No one is able to place limits on how God will act to reconcile the world through Christ. The church can proclaim one avenue of God's revealment with great conviction because of personal experience. As the apostle Paul reminds us in I Corinthians 12, the church is the body of Christ on earth—Christ's resurrected body. Therefore, through the ministries of the church, the intentions of God for the human species are made known in every era.

The church as a whole is called to perform the prophetic function of making God's mind and will known to the nations. The role of leadership in the church facilitates the church's calling and tasks. Leadership for the Reorganized Church of Jesus Christ of Latter Day Saints is focused in the priesthood organization of Aaronic and Melchisedec ministries, a highly diversified division of labor emerging out of the human need for meaningful structure. This pattern of priesthood is designed to enhance the witnessing and redeeming ministry of the gospel. As II Corinthians 5:18 and 19 suggest, not only has God reconciled us to the divine reality through Jesus Christ, but beyond that, God has committed unto those who are reconciled the ministry of reconciliation, to be extended to others in Christian service. This is the heart of Christ's call to all the ministers of the church.

The organizational structure of priesthood in the Restoration movement is unique among the Christian family of churches and denominations. It is important to affirm that Jesus Christ is at the center of all priesthood considerations, even though the terms Aaronic and Melchisedec are most prominent. In a church that affirms that all are called to Christian discipleship and some in the body are further called to leadership responsibilities, it would be well to understand the scriptural background and historical development of the priesthood offices and their interrelationships.

Melchizedek* is a mysterious figure who appears briefly in the text of Genesis for only a few verses (Genesis 14:17–20 IV / 14:18–20 others). He is the king of Salem (probably Jerusalem) and the priest of *El Elyon*, the "most high God." He greets Abraham on his return from battle against four Babylonian kings, offers him bread and wine, blesses Abraham, and receives from him a tenth of the plunder taken in battle.

In later times, Melchisedec assumed a reputation of greatness and grandeur based on the reverence shown by Abraham. Talmudic scholars for centuries have sought for clues as to the nature and character of this shadowy figure in Hebrew history. The Talmud suggests that Melchisedec was really Shem, son of Noah and survivor of the flood. By the time of Abraham, Shem was earth's oldest living person. The name "Melchizedek" in Hebrew can be translated as "king of righteousness" or "my king is Zedek" with Zedek possibly being the name of an ancient Canaanite deity. The figure of Melchisedec combined the offices of king and priest into a prototype that many rulers and ecclesiastical leaders in Israelite history sought to emulate. A succession of priest-kings reigned in Jerusalem, of whom Melchisedec is perhaps the best-known representative.

The only other reference to Melchisedec in the Old Testament comes from Psalm 110:4 in which the person to whom the psalm is addressed is promised, "Thou art a priest forever after the order of Melchizedek." Some rabbinic scholars identified the subject of this psalm to be the Messiah who would come to save the people, a Messiah whose priesthood would be eternal. Other scholars simply believed that Melchisedec stood for a prototype of the ideal ruler of the city of Jerusalem, a flattering image that many kings of the city would aspire to achieve.[1] The role of Melchisedec in the New Testament is dealt with only in the Epistle to the Hebrews. The author of this letter is intent on interpreting the role of Jesus

---

* The Reorganization most commonly uses the Greek spelling "Melchisedec," which generally will be employed here for consistency, rather than the Hebrew "Melchizedek."

Christ in the salvation of humanity. The author uses the references to Melchisedec from Genesis and Psalms to bring the readers to the perfect priest, who is Jesus Christ, of whom Melchisedec was seen to be a faintly glimmering harbinger in the distant past.

The logic seemed incontrovertible to the author of Hebrews. The priest-king Melchisedec serves as proof of the existence of another order of priesthood beyond the Levitical priesthood of the Jewish faith—an order that was older and superior to the Levitical priesthood and its laws. The Melchisedec priesthood antedated the Levitical priesthood by some six hundred years.

After all, Melchisedec was recognized by Abraham to be superior to himself by virtue of receiving a blessing from him and offering a tithe of the spoils of war to him. If Abraham was inferior to Melchisedec, then so was Levi and, by extension, the Levitical priesthood.

The author of Hebrews goes on to affirm that Christ combined the office of king and priest as did Melchisedec. In this sense, Jesus' priesthood was of a different order from that of the Levites, which was temporal and temporary, and was instead after the order of Melchisedec, an eternal priesthood not based on proper genealogy but rather displayed in the power of an endless life and ministry.

The text of the Hebrews letter in the original Greek retells the story from Genesis and then affirms in a mysterious passage that Melchisedec was without mother or father or genealogy and has neither beginning of days nor end of life. This peculiar affirmation stems from the nature of the early rabbinic arguments that were based on the premise that what is *not* said is as significant as what is said in the sacred text. Because there is an absence of information about Melchisedec's lineage and nothing is reported about his death, the silence must be deliberate. And so Melchisedec lives on as a priest forever in Jewish tradition.

In offering his commentary on the text, Joseph Smith Jr. amended the text to say that Melchisedec was ordained a priest after the order of the Son of God, and it is the *priesthood* that is without father or mother, not Melchisedec (Hebrews 7:3).

In any event, the point is clear: priesthood is permanent and the sacrifice of Christ on the cross was offered once and for all on our behalf. The superiority of Christ's priestly offerings over those of Levi's descendants does away with the need for animal sacrifice forever.

For Latter Day Saints the witness of the Book of Mormon supports this view of priesthood, particularly in Alma 9–10. In speaking of ordaining priests after God's holy order, it is affirmed that this holy order existed from the foundation of the world, without beginning of days or end of years. Melchisedec is mentioned as one who was a high priest after this same order, and a compliment is paid to him in that "There were many before him, and also there were many afterwards, but none were greater..." (Alma 10:15). But the main affirmation sounds with brilliant clarity: the priesthood is grounded in the Son of God, and in Christ is to be found the validation for Melchisedec ministry.

Despite the fact that biblical and Book of Mormon references to Melchisedec ministries are brief and inconclusive, a rich system of priesthood organization blossomed and flourished under the direction of Joseph Smith Jr.

In Restoration History

The development of the church priesthood in general, and the Melchisedec order specifically, must be understood in the context of the early church organization. Joseph Smith Jr., blessed with a rich, vivid imagination, created a structural form for the priesthood based on the contemporary needs of the church. That he envisioned a priesthood structure that has withstood the test of time is a testament to his responsiveness to the divine mind and his ability to meet the needs of an emerging church.

Our present priesthood structure, composed of two orders, Aaronic and Melchisedec, has its Restoration origins in the spiritual encounter of Joseph Smith Jr. and Oliver Cowdery with angelic messengers near Harmony, Pennsylvania, in the spring of 1829. In an October 1834 letter to William W. Phelps, published in the Kirtland, Ohio, *Latter Day Saints' Messenger and Advocate*, Oliver Cowdery offered the first written account of that experience. Cowdery recounted that he and Joseph felt the need to be baptized, and that they were concerned because no existing church had proper authority to administer that sacrament. While these events were occurring, the two men translated III Nephi, which discussed the importance of baptism and remission of sins.[2] Oliver described the sequence of events: hearing the voice of the Redeemer speaking peace; an angelic messenger delivering the keys of the gospel of repentance; and then, under the hand of the angel, both men receiving the holy priesthood and priesthood authority in the name of the Messiah.[3]

Though Joseph's account of the experience generally agreed with Oliver's, the young prophet gave many more details in his official history published nearly eight years later in the Nauvoo, Illinois, *Times and Seasons*. Smith stated the specific date of the encounter as May 15, 1829. He identified the messenger as John the Baptist, and the newly conferred priesthood order after Aaron, which holds the keys to the ministering of angels, and the gospel of repentance (neither account identified the specific priesthood office, but only to the Aaronic priesthood order). Upon receiving the Aaronic priesthood, they were commanded to baptize each other, Joseph being baptized first. Next, Joseph ordained Oliver to the Aaronic priesthood, then Oliver ordained Joseph. Then, according to Joseph, John the Baptist claimed that he acted under the authority of Peter, James, and John (three of Jesus' apostles), who held the keys of the Melchisedec priesthood, which would be conferred in due time. The messenger identified Joseph as the first elder and Oliver the second.[4]

The exact beginning of the Melchisedec order is a matter of historical debate. Some have argued, using the Doctrine and Covenants, that Joseph and Oliver received the Melchisedec priesthood during their experience with John the Baptist.[5] Others argue that Joseph and Oliver ordained each other at the time of church organization on April 6, 1830, after receiving a supporting vote of those attending.[6] John Corrill, third church historian, in 1839 wrote of the important June 3, 1831, General Conference in Kirtland, Ohio. In his description of the meeting, he wrote that a pentecostal rush of the Holy Spirit preceded the establishment of the "Melchizedek" (Corrill's spelling) priesthood for the first time.[7] Documentary support for these early references to the origins of the Melchisedec priesthood is no longer extant. But, if the accounts of Joseph and Oliver are relatively accurate, it suggests that priesthood ministry was restored almost a full year before the official church organization and that priesthood offices and responsibilities were not yet well defined.

Specific priesthood offices and the relationship between the two orders evolved over the next several years. Shortly after Joseph arrived in Kirtland, he appointed Edward Partridge to be the church's first bishop through revelation on February 4, 1831.[8] Initiation of the office of high priest occurred in the June 1831 Kirtland Conference when twenty-two elders and one priest were ordained under the direction of the young prophet. Joseph Smith ordained the first five, and Lyman Wight ordained the others. The relationship of two priesthood orders was established by September 1832 when bishops and elders were described as appendages to the "high" or Melchisedec priesthood in the same way that teachers and deacons were considered appendages to the "lesser" Aaronic priesthood.[9]

Particular duties of each priesthood office evolved over time, in similar manner as the two priesthood orders. Sections 17 and 104 of the Doctrine and Covenants demonstrates this evolution. In the spring of 1830 when Section 17 was first recorded, there were no Melchisedec high priests, bishops, or even high councils. In the revised text of 1835 these important offices are mentioned revealing a greater understanding of the different offices and duties. Also found in Section 17 is a statement of need for the vote of the membership in support of the call to priesthood ministry.[10]

In preparation for their first missionary venture, the newly chosen Council of Twelve Apostles asked Joseph Smith for a clarification of their responsibilities as traveling ministers. They received far more than what they requested. Given in Kirtland, Ohio, on March 28, 1835, Section 104 was the most complete explanation yet of Melchisedec (and Aaronic) priesthood responsibility. Again, it reflects greater enlightenment and brings together into one statement, the nature, relationships, and roles of the two priesthood orders.

Moving into the Reorganization period, few changes occurred in the Melchisedec order. In *The True Latter Day Saints' Herald*, Editor Joseph Smith III wrote a series of articles titled "History of the Priesthood." He explored the biblical context for priesthood and basically reaffirmed the prevailing Melchisedec priesthood structure.[11] One notable change that developed over time was the reinterpretation of Melchisedec ministry in the office of evangelist-patriarch. Joseph Smith III placed considerable emphasis on the evangelical ministry of the patriarch.[12]

Moving toward the modern day, less emphasis has been placed on the patriarchal blessing as a clairvoyant statement of a person's future life and more "in the larger context of life, and in terms of perspective and commitment...".[13] Subtle changes have been seen with the addition of female participation in formal ministerial functions and the need to place even greater emphasis on the evangelical role of the Melchisedec office.[14] Reminding the 1996 World Conference that Frederick Madison Smith considered the ecclesiastical titles of patriarch and evangelist as interchangeable, and recognizing the enormous contribution of women in the quorum, in their report to the 1996 World Conference, the Order of Evangelists requested that the church call them "evangelists" and refer to the sacramental prayer as the evangelist's blessing.[15]

Another significant change in the Melchisedec priesthood occurred in the interpretation of who could be ordained to the office of seventy. The Restoration origin of the office of seventy emerged from those who participated in the Zion's Camp march in the spring and summer of 1834. The march occurred at a time when Joseph searched for talent to fill the apostolic and seventy quorums. Nearly all the apostles and seventies ordained in the next year proved their commitment to the church in future service by participating in the march.

During the early and middle years of the Reorganization, the issue of church appointment in seventy ministry developed because of dwindling financial reserves, especially during the difficult 1920s. As a partial solution to the problem, Frederick Madison Smith recommended that seventies should be ordained from the ranks of the self-sustaining ministry, but his proposal did not receive support of the leading quorums of the church. Israel A. Smith raised the issue again in the 1954 biennial gathering by presenting an inspired document admonishing the Council of Presidents of Seventy not to be "overcareful in selecting elders, under the law, to occupy as Seventies."[16] An emotional debate on the conference floor ensued.[17] Though the document finally gained the support of the delegates as the "mind and will of God," the council delayed implementation until the early 1960s when the first self-sustaining seventies were ordained into service, and then only in very small numbers. In the most recent decades, a dramatic reinterpretation, again brought on by budget cuts and high-level decisions directing appointees to administrative responsibilities, resulted in the office of seventy being occupied almost totally by self-sustaining ministers.[18]

Though times and circumstances have changed, it is still possible to recognize most of the same characteristics and functions of Melchisedec ministry established during the early years of the Restoration movement. Driven by the dual forces of revelation and pragmatism, tradition has filled in the gaps in the documentary evidence supporting our priesthood organization. The purposes of meeting human needs, supervising the sacramental functions, and providing administrative leadership are still in place.

In the Congregation

What has been the experience of Melchisedec priesthood ministry in the congregations? Any statement would likely be true for some people and not true for others. Its positive aspects have been tarnished by inadequacies and excesses. Its negative aspects have been overshadowed by inspiration and devotion. How this ministry is experienced may be modified by place and culture, by personal expectation and past experience, by needs and size of congregation, by age and needs of individuals. For some there has been personal kingdom building and for others humble servanthood in the kingdom of God.

Some would understand and experience that Melchisedec ministry should happen outside the congregation—in reaching out beyond sanctuary boundaries. Others' experiences tell them that this ministry is primarily within the congregation through pastoral leadership. Some would see their role to do this or that task, while others would see themselves empowering others to do those same tasks. Some have experienced visionary leadership ministry; for others it has been managerial, inspirational, challenging, or comforting.

In North America a style of congregational leadership developed that rested in the hands of the priesthood and, depending on numbers, primarily the Melchisedec priesthood. An issue of *Priesthood and Leaders Journal* in 1963[19] suggested the use of the branch council as a means of lightening the load of the "branch president." The first suggested form of this council was the elders of the congregation. Smaller congregations would have a council of both Aaronic and Melchisedec priesthood or one made up of departmental heads. In another *Priesthood and Leaders Journal*,[20] the title emphasizes the role of branch president as "coordinator of priesthood." In many congregations the priesthood would meet regularly as a body—probably once a month—and frequently in conversational and council groupings. These meetings would determine what was important for the congregation and which member of the priesthood would be in charge.

What evolved was a team approach to congregational leadership that involved primarily the elders. In the book, *The Ministry of the Elder*, the role of elders is emphasized: "The word 'pastor' is used to include the responsibilities and services of all the elders in a group.... All elders are called to be pastors over the flock."[21]

This system provided a clearly defined way for the leadership function of the congregation to be carried out. Everyone knew and understood their role. It was clear and understandable for all and could be supported by latter-day scripture.[22] Of course, this description overlooks the more subtle influences of members of the congregation who had what we might call an authority of competence and who might have power to influence decisions on the front end or in whether the decisions were carried out successfully to completion. Those who were not elders were forced to find what sometimes appeared to be subversive ways to have voice in the church.

The societal currents in the sixties and seventies began to chip away at this arrangement. The riots and revolution of the late sixties questioned the whole idea of authority at many levels: family, school, church, government. After the cohesiveness of institutions based on authority weakened, the self-potentializing influence that followed moved institutions to become more democratic, including the church. The call found in the Doctrine and Covenants that "All are called according to the gifts of God unto them..."[23] began to have special meaning and members wanted ways to express their giftedness through their congregations.

These influences from society set the stage for the Faith to Grow program of the 1980s which provided for every member to have a role in planning congregational goals, provided opportunities for the unordained to participate in worship planning and participation, and established other congregational planning through commissions. Many congregations embraced it from the beginning with a simple "of course" and some resisted it for what it was—a change in the way congregational leadership had been done in congregations for some time.

Closely following the change in congregational structure was the document presented to the 1984 World Conference which allowed for the ordination of women.[24] Various reactions followed this announcement. For many the announcement was unexpected; for others there was a spirit of anticipation about what new dimensions of ministry this might bring.

The Swiss physician and psychologist Paul Tournier wrote about a gift many women have which he called the "gift of feeling," or a "sense of the person." In 1979 he wrote about the hope often expressed about the ordination of women. He compared the Western world's dominance by reason as the basis for decisions and actions with the Eastern world's more rounded approach, which includes emotions. He expressed the hope that as women move into positions of leadership, they will infuse societies' structures with their special talent—the gift of feeling. He writes,

> I believe that women have a mission today. Men have kept them out of public life and have built up our Western technical civilization without them—a masculine society, ordered entirely in accordance with masculine values, and tragically lacking the contribution women could make.[25]

Before the ordination of women, this same hope was expressed. Now, after more than a decade since women were ordained, many lament that not as much has changed as was hoped. It may be true that ordained women are functioning much as they have seen modeled by the priesthood throughout their church life. It may also be true that such changes are subtle and difficult to measure. Perhaps the whole movement from congregational power and authority resting primarily in the Melchisedec priesthood to the wider participation of members of the congregation not only made it possible for women to be ordained, but it created congregations that are more sensitive to the needs of all people, including everyone's need to offer their gifts in the kingdom of God. Women have moved quite naturally into the parts of Melchisedec ministry such as pastoral care and worship that call for the sensitive, gentler side of human nature, which reminds people to bring the gift of sensitivity into all parts of the elder's ministry.

Before the changes in the 1980s, not only administrative but worship leadership was solely the responsibility of the elders. Thomas R. Beil wrote in 1961: "Responsibility for ordering the service of worship rests with the eldership of the church..."[26] while referencing Doctrine and Covenants 17:9 that "The elders are to conduct the meetings as they are led by the Holy Ghost, according to the commandments and revelations of God." Besides worship services being planned by the elders, priesthood were the only ones to lead the worship, outside of participants in music. In some congregations this meant that only priesthood could stand in certain places and walk through certain doors. One congregation determined that the choir could not sing on Communion Sunday because the choir included women.

While some have lamented the loss of "authority" by the Melchisedec priesthood, many see an important shift from using such authority to tend to the functions of the congregation to tending to the spiritual needs and potential of people. The spiritual nurture of individuals and groups is a challenging task, one that depends on the spiritual maturity and sensitivity of the minister and follows the model of our mentor, Jesus Christ, who built the kingdom in the hearts of people.

What has not changed is that priesthood members serve as agents of grace to offer a symbolic channel for the Holy Spirit to touch human need. Floyd M. McDowell wrote of this challenge to not forget

> ...the soul-stirring responsibility of speaking for God and Christ to the people and that of representing them to God and Christ. What a heart tug. Even yet the thought of such a responsibility overwhelms me. It seemed for a time that I wouldn't be able to take it. Surely I am unworthy of such a ministry. Memory of that heart tug, memory of those moments of humility and anguish of soul has never left me. As a minister I must never let go of the hand of those I would serve. As a minister I must never let go of the hand of the Master.[27]

Ministers are looked to for this awesome role. To illustrate, an elderly lady in preparation for surgery asked for administration. The following day after surgery she said, "Whenever I began to feel apprehensive, I remembered the feel of the elders' hand and, remembering that he stood in the stead of Christ, I felt Christ's holding my hand and was comforted."

The church has come to this point in time with guidance and models from scriptures, a history of evolving priesthood ministries, and models of Melchisedec ministry today. What it means to be an elder in the new millennium is yet to be discovered—and that can happen only in the presence and direction of the Holy Spirit.

Notes

1. Talmud, Nedarim 32b; compare also Sanhedrin 108b.
2. Neither Smith nor Cowdery referred to a specific verse, but III Nephi 3:67–70 may well be what prompted their concern.
3. *Latter Day Saints' Messenger and Advocate* 1, no. 1 (October 1834): 15–16.
4. Joseph Smith Jr., "History of Joseph Smith," *Times and Seasons* 3, no. 19 (August 1, 1842): 865–866.
5. Doctrine and Covenants 16:3b and 26:2d–3a.
6. Joseph Smith [III] and Heman C. Smith, *The History of the Reorganized Church of Jesus Christ of Latter Day Saints*, Vol. 1, 1805–1835 (Independence, Missouri: Herald House, 1952), 63–66, 76–77.
7. John Corrill, *A Brief History of the Church of Christ of Latter Day Saints (commonly called Mormons); Including an Account of Their Doctrine and Discipline; With the Reasons of the Author for Leaving the Church* (St. Louis, Missouri: printed for the author, 1839), chapter 10. Vault Collection, RLDS Library-Archives. It is important to note that the author may be using the term "Melchizedek" proleptically. This occurs when a person uses a term common to his contemporary setting, but not used in the era to which it is referred.
8. Doctrine and Covenants 41:3c.
9. Doctrine and Covenants 83:5.
10. Richard P. Howard, *Restoration Scriptures: A Study of Their Textual Development*, 2nd ed. (Independence, Missouri: Herald House, 1995), 158–160.
11. For example *The True Latter Day Saints' Herald* (July 15, 1863) and (September 1, 1863) and (September 15, 1863).
12. Doctrine and Covenants 125:3–6.
13. Reed M. Holmes, "Report to the First Presidency and the World Conference," *World Conference Bulletin* (1976): 48.
14. For the first time, in their 1984 report to the World Conference, the priesthood order identified themselves as the Order of Evangelist-Patriarchs; also, in the same report, they announced the distribution of an important brochure titled, "Introduction to the Ministry of the Evangelist-Patriarch," *World Conference Bulletin* (1984): 60. From 1988 to the present, each significant statement to the church during the World Conferences has been addressed from the Order of Evangelists. Interestingly, the presidents of the quorum retained their title as presiding patriarch until 1994 when Paul W. Booth took the title presiding evangelist. It is worth noting that Elbert A. Smith generally preferred the latter title.
15. Everett S. Graffeo, "Report to the First Presidency and the World Conference," *World Conference Bulletin* (1996): 81.
16. Doctrine and Covenants 143:3a.
17. Though a majority of the Council of Twelve and the Council of the Presidents of Seventy supported the first two paragraphs of Section 143, they called into question the divinity of paragraph 3. The Conference delegates rejected a motion for referral to a Joint Council of the First Presidency, the Council of Twelve, and the Council of Presidents of Seventy, and eventually approved the document in its entirety. After the vote, speaking for the Council of Presidents of Seventy, Zenas Z. Renfroe pledged the support of the two councils because "the conference voted to accept it as the mind and will of the Lord." See *A Transcript of the Business Sessions: The 1954 General Conference*, Reorganized Church of Jesus Christ of Latter Day Saints, The Auditorium, Independence, Missouri, Produced by The Department of History, 1971, Saturday, April 10, 1954, Business Session, 111–122.
18. As of this writing, there are 250 seventies in the seven quorums of which only ten are under church appointment.
19. Gerald Kruse, "Using the Branch Council," *Priesthood and Leaders Journal* (February 1963): 1–3, 34.

20. Melvin E. Francis, "Branch President: Co-ordinator of Priesthood," *Priesthood and Leaders Journal* (Summer 1961): 48–51.
21. Dwight D. W. Davis, *The Ministry of the Elder: A Manual for Priesthood Study and Reference* (Independence, Missouri: Herald Publishing House, 1953), 108.
22. An example is found in Doctrine and Covenants 43:4.
23. See Doctrine and Covenants 119:8b.
24. Doctrine and Covenants 156.
25. Paul Tournier, *The Gift of Feeling* (Atlanta, Georgia: John Knox Press, 1979), 1.
26. Thomas R. Beil, "Who Shall Plan the Service of Worship?" *Priesthood and Leaders Journal* (April 1961): 9.
27. Floyd M. McDowell, "You Stand Between...," *Priesthood and Leaders Journal* (April 1963): 39.

Chapter 2

The Elder: A Unique Appendage

Larry McGuire

Most of us have an idea of what the duties and responsibilities are of the office of elder. Our understanding may have come from studying materials written concerning this office. Others may have developed an understanding by watching elders performing their ministerial tasks. Regardless of how we have come to understand the elder's duties and responsibilities, we need to look again at this office: an office central to the life of a community of worshipers. Before I address the specifics of the office of elder, let me present a few thoughts concerning ministry in general.

Each of us takes seriously our roles as member, leader, pastor, or priesthood. We struggle with whether or not our efforts are faithful to God's call for our lives. We wrestle with keeping things moving, stable, in balance, fresh, and exciting. All of this "keeping" in a community of faith pushes each person to evaluate what needs to be kept and what needs to be put aside. Evaluation in ministry needs to be done consistently and constantly. The drain to strive for excellence can cause some to lose perspective of the ideal of being faithful to God's call.

> Excellence in ministry is not a one-person show. Even with vigorous and dynamic pastoral leadership, long-term excellence in faithfully carrying out the mission of the Gospel occurs only where [people] are committed to the vision of what their congregation's ministry can be. In the excellent churches, the [people] "own," take responsibility for and are trusted with carrying out the work of the people of God.[1]

The reality is that ministry is and must be mutual. All people of a community work together to celebrate God's acts in their lives today, to be ministers of encouragement to people who are confronted with a loss of hope, and to be transition people in the lives of those who suffer from past hurts and desperately want to stop the circle of abuse and pain. That is the true meaning of covenant. We become bound together through Jesus Christ, and we share in mutual partnership to be faithful in witness and mission to God's people.

Liturgy means "the work of the people." This definition brings new light to the apostle Paul's concept of the priesthood of all believers. It calls each of us to be actively engaged in ministry—all people, not just those set apart to proclaim the Word and participate in the sacraments. With all engaged in ministry, the hope and vision of being ministers of God's grace becomes a reality. No one is left out! We are all connected through our covenant, and we are strengthened by shouldering together to share in ministry.

This is not a new concept for Christian service. Consider these familiar terms that are common in a theological discussion: *kerygma* (the Word proclaimed), *koinonia* (Christ-centered fellowship and devotion), or *diakonia* (ministry to the community in need). This idea of all participating in ministry is not new. Unfortunately, the reality in today's communities of faith is that participation by all is not the norm; it is the exception. This begs the idea of all being accountable for what takes place in their faith community's experience. We will be greatly enhanced as a body by each of the parts working together in mission and celebration. It strengthens the body of Christ to have all functioning in useful, fulfilling ways.

Daniel L. Migliore presents several interesting concepts in his book *Faith Seeking Understanding*. One of his chapters addresses the issue of proclamation, sacraments, and ministry. Consider the following:

> ...that all Christians are called to the worship and service of the triune God. All are given the vocation of love of God and love of neighbor, all are called to follow Jesus Christ and to be his faithful witnesses in word and deed, all are given gifts by the Spirit to make their unique contribution to the life of the community and its mission to the world.[2]

This is his definition in a broad sense for the need and meaning of ordained ministry. He does discuss a narrow meaning that relates to proclamation and sacrament. Migliore goes on to state very clearly that, "The authority of the ordained minister is based not on his or her person but solely on the gospel of Jesus Christ. It is an authority that is always exercised in partnership with the whole people of God. Ministerial authority is not monarchical but collegial in nature."[3] This addresses the concern I have heard and, unfortunately, witnessed in the actions of some: that priesthood is not a right of domination and control. It is an expression of gifts and responding to a sense of God's call. When priesthood is viewed as a way to control, the covenant is not enhanced. In fact, there is nothing mutual in domination, only authority over something or someone. The ministry of priesthood must be that of mutual benefit and expression of God's gifts to each of us.

Priesthood is something bigger than we are. It connects us to God in a relationship that causes us to examine who we are and realize whose we are. We have been called by God, and God has called us by name to be engaged in a covenantal relationship as servant ministers who stand in the stead of Jesus Christ. There are times of challenge, times of questioning, times of doubt, times of joy and excitement, and each time is an opportunity for reflection and renewal. If we acknowledge that we are called to ministry, we acknowledge that it is not something of our own creation but comes as a gift, an expression of something that is beyond ourselves. We are responding to a call to service that requires us to be connected in an intimate way.

The awesome thought of standing in the stead of Christ must cause us to look beyond ourselves and serve a greater purpose. We choose and are chosen to serve God. The specifics of calling are diverse, and our experiences are so different that to define God's call in a specific way is impossible. The examples found in the scriptures record a variety of ways that God's call took place. The common idea is that people were chosen, and then they chose to respond to what they considered to be God's call. We are no different, and our experience is no less valid. God acts and we respond as best we can.

Mrs. Gulensky is a second-grade teacher in Columbus, Ohio. One day while I was visiting with Bruce Crockett, an appointee friend of mine, he relayed to me what Mrs. Gulensky had shared with the students in her class. She said, "Don't look at people as disabled; rather, look at people as differently abled." I have not forgotten that statement, and in preparing for this chapter, her statement continued to come to mind. The office of elder is a unique office that finds itself expressed most often within a local congregation or mission. The qualities of an elder are vast and diverse. All priesthood offices call for our singular gifts, and they require the combination of personality and talents that are uniquely ours. Our experiences and our background in life are also key in developing our ministry.

For as in one body we have many members, and not all the members have the same function, so we, who are many, are one body in Christ, and individually we are members one of another. We have gifts that differ according to the grace given to us....—Romans 12: 4–6 NRSV

The people in our congregations depend on each person to share their gifts, and such sharing can strengthen and enhance that community. This is best summed up by, "If one member suffers, all suffer together with it; if one member is honored, all rejoice together with it" (I Corinthians 12: 26 NRSV). The components of each priesthood office are dependent on each other.

The office of elder is different from the other offices and yet has similar responsibilities and qualities. "There is no difference in the importance of various priesthood roles, although there are differences in the offices in which one is to act."[4] However, the office of elder is considered an appendage to the high priesthood. An appendage is defined as something that is an external organ or an accompaniment. I have come to understand that the office of elder is anything but that. In the life of our church, elders are considered the central leaders and shepherds in most communities. Generally, elders offer ministry in established congregations and missions. Their ministry is usually identified as attached to that area and is not considered an appendage.

> All ministry grows out of the elder's responsibility to strengthen the faith of the people and to encourage, nurture, and sustain them....
>
> ...The elder is called upon to preach faith, repentance, remission of sins, and reception of the Holy Spirit among the people. The elder is to be an evangelist, calling all to come to Christ and teaching them the gospel.... Elders are to call people to a sense of their destiny as a new humanity and as citizens of the kingdom of God.[5]

Each of these areas is designed to bring hope to people and to edify them in their journey with God. Notice that the function of the elder is not limited to presiding as pastor or in worship. In fact, that is one very small part of the potential for expression of their ministry.

A significant portion of ministry for the office of elder involves some type of evangelistic effort. People are not *just* elders who might have an evangelistic spirit or the spirit of invitation. Integral to the ministry of the elder is to be involved in inviting people to come to Christ. Diligence needs to be given in supporting elders to expand their role beyond the presiding function. In the case of a high priest being present in a congregation, they are called to fulfill that function. Envision elders as ministers of mission engaged in expansion opportunities for a congregation. By having the elders engaged in evangelistic efforts, the Aaronic ministers could be empowered to offer supportive and valuable home ministry to those being invited to come and be a part of the fellowship.

The functions listed throughout the Doctrine and Covenants give us an indication that elders, regardless of where they serve, are integral to the spiritual life of people. The focus of ministry for an elder is concerned with expansion and being ministers of grace. The elder's responsibility to call people into a sense of destiny and purpose in the kingdom of God is an awesome task. The unique task is found in having a relationship with people and an understanding of the needs of people. The key is found in relationships that are based on the covenant mentioned earlier: the idea of mutual benefit for the people of God. The role of mentoring others to offer ministry is also an important dimension of being an elder. The opportunity to share and assist in the development of others' gifts and ministry is not limited to an elder, nor to priesthood. The opportunity to mentor is considered one of stewardship. Elders, indeed all ministers, are often confronted with having limited time to serve. The need to train and develop others to offer their gifts is crucial to ensuring the long-term health and growth of a congregation.

Elders assist in developing a congregational life that is unique. As elders serve the needs of people within a congregation, they are also called to represent Jesus Christ and the church within their community. They are called to be frontline representatives of Jesus Christ to the community and to invite others to come and join them in that task.

A quick review of a plan for serving as an elder includes twenty ways to accomplish this task. Emphasis is not limited to the daily tasks of congregational life. Often elders are expected to concentrate on ministry to the members and are not free to be engaged in the ministry of invitation to the community. I am convinced that if the eldership were encouraged and provided opportunities to be involved as missionaries, the church would experience a renewed spirit of evangelism and witness a time of great expansion.

Another key to this idea is that elders need to give Aaronic ministers and the members themselves the opportunity to function as mentors and ministers to those being introduced to the fellowship through this renewed force of frontline evangelists. Too often the opportunity for all to be involved in discipleship is left up to those who are inviting and bringing new people to the fellowship. I am certain that if the team concept were implemented in congregations, the fear of territory would diminish. When possible, with high priests presiding over a congregation, elders working as evangelists in the community and offering supportive ministry within the congregation, Aaronic members fulfilling the role of nurturers and family advocates, and members actively engaged in inviting their friends to come and be a part of our community of faith and fulfilling their role as living expressions of God's grace would be a powerful presence in the places where we live and work. If all these parts function together, the potential for growth is limitless.

We need hope. We need a sense that there is something bigger than ourselves at work in our world and that there is some meaning and purpose to all that we encounter. Elders, working in the community and in the local congregation, can be instrumental as bearers of hope. They are called to share the reality that God's love has transformed our lives and the lives of others. This sharing brings new hope, meaning, and a sense of direction that gives each of us hope. Elders as bearers of hope bring the confirmation that God continues to be at work. As servant leaders for God, elders are also called to provide visionary leadership: a ministry of what can be achieved by faithful witness. This is the idea of hope for tomorrow. It requires a boldness in witness and discipleship. The development of future ministry can cause a great deal of stress for members of the congregation. The realities of change threaten the safety that some cherish in their congregational life. Hope for tomorrow should not be viewed as destruction of the present and past. Indeed, visionary leadership is required of all. We are called on to proclaim hope and that proclamation comes in the form of Jesus Christ.

> If you have the gift of leadership, God ignites in your heart a vision. You cannot *not* talk about it. There is so much power released when leaders start casting a godly vision. It draws people out of the woodwork. It gets bored spectators out onto the playing field.[6]

The compelling vision is key to the success of the mission. We also need to remember that visions have a reality and consequence. Elders are given the unique opportunity to be engaged in that vision—modeling it for a congregation and mentoring others to join in the identified ministry. Earlier I mentioned the scriptural reference to elders being a unique appendage to the office of high priest. The reason this office serves as an appendage is that it exemplifies the unique relationship all priesthood has to *the* high priest, Jesus Christ.

Our call to ministry, regardless of office, is to signal that God is at work in creation. Our acceptance of being called to a specific priesthood office is a recognition of our being blessed with unique gifts and talents. We are asked to express those gifts through service. We are also given the responsibility of fostering growth and further development of those gifts, which is responsible stewardship. We are called to be practitioners of our faith, not for ourselves but for the community of faith we represent.

As elders continue to be ministers of hope and assist in the expansion of the church, the blessings we will find as a faith community will be in winning others to Christ. We serve others—encountering events and circumstances that require us to reach beyond ourselves to the source of all hope. The ministry of Jesus Christ needs the talents and gifts of people. People who are willing to respond with passion and compassion will meet the challenges of today. Elders are but one source of ministry who can offer the necessary perspective to people searching for hope. Elders engaged in community and in congregations face an awesome task of living in the tension between the needs of the people outside the walls of our churches and needs of those inside.

We experience God's presence through responding to the call placed before us. Our individual gifts are to help us bring ministry to those in need. People holding the office of elder are unique and their ministry is necessary to bring wholeness and hope to a hurting world. The burden of being a bridge and a lighthouse is not an easy task. Elders are called and gifted to do both. Being a bridge from the congregation to the members of the community is vital. We need to grasp opportunities to be active in causes and organizations that are promoting the worth of people. Elders are to be a lighthouse, not only to the community at large, but also to friends and members. The quality and integrity of congregational life is directly linked to the ministry of elders—they have a profound role to lead our congregations around the globe.

The office of elder is unique in our faith. Elders, like each of us, are called to be living expressions of Jesus Christ. Their affirmative witness not only inspires new people to come to Christ, but also inspires congregation members to be engaged in the same cause. The challenge is for elders to be faithful in proclaiming Christ and be advocates to the communities where they live, work, and worship that God is not finished with us yet. We must be bold in our witness of God's grace and invite others to come and share.

Notes

1. Daniel V. Biles, *Pursuing Excellence in Ministry* (Washington, D.C.: The Alban Institute, 1988), 9.
2. Daniel L. Migliore, *Faith Seeking Understanding: An Introduction to Christian Theology* (Grand Rapids, Michigan: Wm. B. Eerdmans, 1991), 227.
3. Ibid., 229.
4. Doctrine and Covenants 129:7.
5. Wayne A. Ham, compiler, PA 104 The Elder (Independence, Missouri: Temple School Center, 1996), 12–13.
6. Bill Hybels, "Up to the Challenge," *Leadership: A Practical Journal for Church Leaders* (Fall 1996): 59.

Chapter 3

The Elder and Function: Servant Ministry

Joni Wilson

The primary function of the office of elder is to proclaim the gospel and provide grace and hope in loving service to all through effective leadership. As the world moves into the twenty-first century, the need is ever greater for people who desire to find meaning and purpose for life. There is a widening chasm between those people who need the basic necessities of life (clean air and water, shelter, food, clothing) and those who have these necessities but crave health, security, safety, love, acceptance, and a purposeful life. The ministry of caring is urgently needed for people on both sides of life as well as those in between. The elder, a minister of caring, is called to be joyful, competent, and compassionate in this expanding technological global society. The purpose of this chapter is to provide principles and guidelines for individual and group use to prepare for effective servant ministry in a world desperate for abundant life.

In the past, the office of elder was primarily one of traditional teaching, preaching, and administration of daily office affairs to those who happened to be attending a service or within their range of leadership. There was a detachment, because often the ministry was one-sided, with the elder giving more as a spectator or observer. A new aspect of the elder's calling is to be involved in the action: to become a part of difficulties, pains, and joys; and to be a participant in proclaiming the gospel. John 15:16 gives the words of Jesus as "Ye have not chosen me, but I have chosen you, and ordained you, that ye should go and bring forth fruit...".

Proclaiming the gospel is looking for opportunities to express the love of God continuously to self, others, community, and the world. The individual must first be ready to reach outward. This may be done through a variety of physical and spiritual disciplines such as study, meditation, prayer, generosity, and fasting. There are disciplines of simplicity, solitude, service, and compassion. The elder also participates in corporate disciplines of confession, worship, celebration, listening, and love.

An elder must become a genuine person. Genuine people truly believe in what they say and do; they cannot be hypocritical. The life of the genuine person reflects his or her true nature. If a person truly wants to serve God, he or she must be willing to toil in the field beside the other laborers: "therefore, if ye have desires to serve God, ye are called to the work, for, behold, the field is white already to harvest" (Doctrine and Covenants 4:1c). The new fields are the pews of the church, the house next door, the streets outside, and the world beyond. An elder must be willing to work in the blistering sun and survive the dangers of the harvest wherever the field is ripe. It means working where the individual's strengths are and working with others to complement and enhance each other's power.

The following story is illustrative of the function of the office of elder:

There once was a wise and beloved king who cared greatly for his people and wanted only what was the best for them. The people knew the king took a personal interest in their affairs and tried to understand how his decisions affected their lives. Periodically, he would disguise himself and wander through the streets, trying to see life from their perspective.

One day he disguised himself as a poor villager and went to visit the public baths. Many people were there enjoying the fellowship and relaxation. The water for the baths was heated by a furnace in the cellar, where one man was responsible for maintaining the comfort level of the water. The king made his way to the basement to visit with the man who tirelessly tended the fire.

The two men shared a meal together, and the king befriended this lonely man. Day after day, week in and week out, the king went to visit the firetender. The man in the cellar soon became close to his strange visitor because he came down to the basement where he was. No one else ever had showed that much caring or concern.

One day the king revealed his true identity to his friend. It was a risky move, for he feared that the man might ask him for special favors or a gift. Instead, the king's new friend looked into his eyes and said, "You left your comfortable palace to sit with me in this hot and dingy cellar. You ate my meager food and genuinely showed you cared about what happens to me. On other people you might bestow rich gifts, but to me you have given the greatest gift of all. You gave me the gift of yourself."[1]

It is tempting simply to preach and teach the gospel as learned from the scriptures. It is easy to recite phrases, dates, names, and parables. It is much more difficult to give of self because the risk is that one will care and become involved. An elder might speak earnestly and passionately in relating the story of the good Samaritan stopping to help a person in need. Will that same elder risk *being* a good Samaritan to help another?

The true essence of the personality of an elder should be that of *peacemaker*. How appropriate that the Temple in Independence is dedicated to the pursuit of peace. But the building itself cannot be the arms and legs that make peace happen. Peacemakers who are servant ministers are needed to provide the outreach. The only time in the New Testament that the Greek term translated "peacemakers" appears is in the Beatitudes (Matthew 5:1–14 IV / 5:1–12 others). The thrust of this scripture is action: Make peace! A peacemaker is involved, passionate, willing to risk, and steps into the needs of others.

> Although attempting to bring about world peace through the internal transformation of individuals is difficult, it is the only way. Wherever I go, I express this, and I am encouraged that people from many different walks of life receive it well. Peace must first be developed within an individual. And I believe that love, compassion, and altruism are the fundamental basis for peace. Once these qualities are developed within an individual, he or she is then able to create an atmosphere of peace and harmony. This atmosphere can be expanded and extended from the individual to his [or her] family, from the family to the community and eventually to the whole world.[2]

There are some things that being a peacemaker does *not* mean:

1. It does not mean avoiding conflict and confrontations. Passivity is walking by or refusing to become involved. A mediator will see signs and symptoms of impending or continuing conflict and help to diffuse and settle differences in an affirming manner for both sides.

2. Being a peacemaker does not mean to be so relaxed as to appear uninterested. Knowledge and wisdom are useful tools in understanding and dealing with others. With evaluation comes the foresight of giving an opinion and remaining silent.

3. Being a peacemaker does not mean all-out peace at any price. Romans 12:18 (NRSV) instructs people: "If it is possible, so far as it depends on you, live peaceably with all." This may mean a compromise or a willingness to let go for another's sake. People often need a sense of control and will fight for their side just for the sake of winning, when perhaps what is more important is a sense of worth for the other person.

Nobody knows what was so important that it caused the Lamanites and Nephites in the Book of Mormon to fight to their deaths. Perhaps the exact divisive event is not named in order to teach those who follow an important lesson. There are similar examples today as seemingly minor issues divide friends, families, and countries. Instead, why not focus on the similarities of people that provide a common ground?

How can elders work to provide grace and hope to others? Turn to the words of Solomon to reaffirm the things peacemakers do:[3]

Peacemakers build up: "The wise woman builds her house..." (Proverbs 14:1, NASB). This may be the physical construction of a house as to structure, location, neighborhood, color scheme, and floor plan. But it is also the provision by men and women of a home environment of love, emotional warmth, and safety where continued learning and growth may occur.

Peacemakers watch their tongues and heal rather than hurt: "A gentle answer turns away wrath.... Pleasant words are...healing" (Proverbs 15:1, 16:24, NASB). Words can be more powerful and inflict more intense and long-lasting pain than any physical wound. How easy it is to give another person praise, lift them up, or show concern. But too often people are critical in their comments, or offer unwanted advice.

Peacemakers are slow to anger: "He who is slow to anger pacifies contention" (Proverbs 15:18, NASB). Anger is an intense emotion that many people have not been taught to control. Thinking about things, cooling off, and waiting are important ways to control anger and channel a response into constructive criticism or a comment that will receive an appropriate response.

Peacemakers are humble and trusting: "...whoever trusts in the Lord will be enriched" (Proverbs 28:25, NRSV). The basic attitude of a peacemaker does not accept the glory but includes others in the celebration. A true leader acknowledges all who participated in the work as a team. An attitude of trust, not innocence or ignorance but one shared with wisdom, is needed in order for the peacemaker to risk.

In a world increasingly torn by stress, loneliness, and isolation, the elder must minister to those in their immediate vicinity. This means family, neighbors, coworkers, and the community. It means giving caring ministry to others regardless of their religion, background, or response. If a person is truly serving without thought of self, all humans become worthy of love and acceptance. The RLDS Church affirms the worth of all people. "Individuals should be fully accepted into the ongoing life of the congregation" (Standing High Council Statement, March 18, 1982). The church also states it will "acknowledge and affirm human diversity... where all persons may find acceptance and the opportunity to share their giftedness" (World Conference Resolution 1226, adopted 1992).

Jesus Christ is the model for a Christian minister to follow. Christ listened compassionately, and people from all walks of life were the object of his love—regardless of social standing, health, or personality. While the model of Christ is a good one to follow, other religions also have reliable models. It is wise to acknowledge the models other people may follow in the world. This enables a minister to reach out with intelligence to share with others in a common bond.

Other models include Buddha, who searched for ways of righteousness. Buddhists today attempt to reach a state of complete peace and love through following steps toward enlightenment. Buddhism states that "One act of pure love in saving life is greater than spending the whole of one's time in religious offerings to the gods...." Confucius led people by an example of high moral principles. He promoted ethics, a sense of balance, and a right perspective on life. Mohammed was a prophet in the Islamic tradition. He taught that all of life is unified and seeks to blend its spiritual and material aspects. The founder of Jainism, Mahavira, taught ethical purity, love, and kindness and that "One should show compassion to all creatures...." Sikhism's version is that "We obtain salvation by loving our fellow beings and God."[5] Followers of the Tao, believed to be written by Lao-tzu, attempt to live a life of humility and harmony.

Christians have much to learn from and to teach others who are in need of the gospel. Understanding other models and backgrounds enhances individual and group ministry. People discover that they share certain principles and can build relationships from that point.

These principles do not indicate to love others passively from afar but to be involved actively in a real, day-to-day participatory love. It does not indicate to just love the people we like, but instead to accept all regardless of differences. Part of the key is to discover the hurts, wants, and frustrations of other people, not what the perceived need may be. We tend to think we know what others' needs are based on *our* personal needs.

A function of the elder is to not only have good intentions but to put the intentions into action. There can be many meetings, well-spoken words, and well-meaning support for theories without any real need being met. A good way to reinforce these actions is to find others attempting to support each other in a team effort to serve. It helps to keep a positive viewpoint about others and not waste time on backbiting and revenge. When joining a community or church activity, it is best to get to know the existing systems and the people's strengths and weaknesses, and then analyze and evaluate the activity for possible improvement.

There may be a tendency to have a "better than you" attitude. Our society is currently built on hierarchies and corporate mind-sets of top to bottom. It is easy to persuade people that some are worth more than others. This mock superiority is not a benefit when attempting to reach out to others. It is also not wise to treat others with a parental attitude, as if to take care of them. The "needy" are people everywhere in a variety of situations. They may be the hungry, homeless, or jobless. But more often they are the lonely, the unfulfilled, and the unloved. People build houses, fill food pantries, and give of time and money, but they do not share as well of their love, time, and purpose.

An elder needs to live carefully. "Not careful as in fearful; but careful as in full of care."[6] Caring for others is an important spiritual act. It can be one of simplicity, such as a shared meal, a kind word, or a prayer. It may also be as simple as pruning a tree, singing a song, holding a hand, or picking up a piece of trash. It is a mistake to overlook the simplest acts of spirituality. Ambition tells people to find spirituality through meditating for hours, fasting for weeks, eating only certain foods, or performing exacting rituals.

The small, ordinary things given from the heart are better. People tend to wish for the extraordinary gift of another so they, too, can give. If a person has good humor, then laughter is the precious gift they give. If another person is a musician, then music is their gift. If one listens well to others, then that is their gift of ministry.

Appropriate ministry occurs when a person is sensitive to the needs of others from the other's point of view. A minister shares in the context of needing the other person as much as the other person needs the minister. Intentionally choosing to walk with others, work with others, live with others, and love others is essential long before becoming concerned with changing others. Such ministry offers hope, joy, and peace to those who view the world as aimless, hopeless, lonely, alienated, filled with confusion, and chaos.[7]

If elders are to express loving service to all, they should open their home, time, talent, and self. This is an abundant expression of the fullness of a life of positive stewardship. God has given the commandment to love others.

We must be willing to listen if we expect to be able to serve. We may offer advice when it is requested but should never impose our ideas on others. We each must make our own course through the fields. When we offer advice, we should consider all who are involved, that everyone can be helped. We are to forgive even before forgiveness is requested, and to love when there is no cause to promote that love.[8]

Learning to listen with the heart is an essential element for providing effective leadership. Sometimes it means stepping out of the traditional role of what is right. The following tale illustrates this: There was

a small village congregation who had gathered together in the House of Prayer on the eve of the High Holy Days. They were waiting for the rabbi to arrive so that the services could begin. Time passed, but he did not come.

One of the women of the congregation began to worry about her little girl whom she'd left alone in the house, so she decided to hurry home to look after her child and to make sure she hadn't wakened.

When she listened at the door of her house, everything was quiet. Softly she turned the knob and put her head into the room—and there stood the rabbi holding her child in his arms. On his way to the House of Prayer, he had heard the child crying and had played with her and sung to her until she fell asleep.[9]

In this "modern" age, one should wonder: Why did the mother leave her child alone? She should be reported to the Child Abuse Hotline. Why did the rabbi enter the house uninvited? He should be arrested for breaking and entering. How would he dare to play with a little girl without someone else present? Again a report has to be made to the Child Abuse Hotline. Did the rabbi sing a politically correct song and was it on key? The musicians and word watchdogs need to know. Why would the rabbi leave his congregation waiting? Obviously this is a breach of contract. But regardless of the consequences—and this is *not* advocating the willful negligence of responsible duty—the point is that the rabbi chose to meet the needs of the moment.

How often do people meet the needs of the moment? It seems more important to be on time, dressed appropriately, say the perfect words, or have the best prepared meal. Again, this is not advocating negligence, but a rethinking of what is most important for meeting the needs of self and others in effective ministry. It means stepping outside the box of the usual way of caring for others.

An important aspect of effective leadership for the coming century and for servant ministry is to think in a new and different way about "common knowledge." Most Christians are very familiar with the Ten Commandments. These commandments provide important moral and ethical foundations for the Christian, Islamic, and Jewish faiths. As stated in the Bible, they serve as warnings. But what if they were turned into positive affirmations?

For example, *You shall not kill* becomes "Heal those who have been harmed." *You shall not steal* becomes "Give more to the world than you take." *You shall not bear false witness* becomes "Respect the dignity of truth." *You shall not covet your neighbor's . . .* becomes "Content yourself with the necessities" (adapted from Exodus 20:13, 15–17).[10] Each statement is turned from passive inactivity and becomes the way of life for a peacemaker. As the elder moves with others into the twenty-first century, the challenge is to meet the needs of the individual. Regardless of the technological wonders that are in the world and those being created, the need will always be there for a loving, caring minister to touch the hearts and souls of humans. Elders in a ministry of caring must be willing to risk. They will not know the ending, but must reach out regardless.

> There was a young man walking down a deserted beach just before dawn. In the distance he saw a frail old man. As he approached the old man, he saw him picking up stranded starfish and throwing them back into the sea. The young man gazed in wonder as the old man again and again threw the small starfish from the sand to the water. He asked him, "Why do you spend so much energy doing what seems to be a waste of time?" The old man explained that the stranded starfish would die if left in the morning sun. "But there must be thousands of beaches and millions of starfish," exclaimed the young man, "How can your effort make any difference?" The old man looked down at the small starfish in his hand and as he threw it to safety in the sea he said, "It makes a difference to this one."[11]

In today's ever-changing world, how does the elder know which way to turn to offer ministry? The media bombards the viewer and reader daily with the injustice and inhumane treatment of humans in the world. People are further alienated from others as they sit in offices filled with electronic wizardry that is marvelous but does not allow human interaction. Conceivably a person might go through an entire day without human contact. Talking on a phone and leaving a message on a voice-mail system, networking on a computer, electronic mail, phoning an order and remembering which button to press for service, listening to a radio or television, banking at automatic teller machines, watching videos or a movie, drive-through fast food, and any other number of "conveniences" certainly provide the background for the withdrawal from contact from other humans.

Where then does a person place his or her priorities? The following principles will help in deciding where to focus energies:

Relax your standards. Live up to your own expectations, not those of others. Arrange for time during every day to be alone and quiet just to give some of your time to you.

Free yourself of stereotypical roles. Divide tasks according to inclination and expertise, not the way it's always been done. Ask for help and delegate as needed.

Take the time to figure out what you find most satisfying about your ministry. Choose a more pleasurable way to accomplish the giving of your gifts. Be realistic about what you can do.

Create time for the things you care about. Make a unique schedule that works for you. This may mean saying no to some requests and making room for others.

Learn to be flexible. Think differently in your expectations and relationships. Explore the options, not the "shoulds."

There are always tips, hints, and ways of doing things better that may allow for a life to be lived more effectively. But individuals must determine for themselves the way they choose to minister. It is a personal attitude and vision of the journey of life. The words of Antoine de Saint-Exupéry in *The Little Prince* perhaps express it best: "It is only with the heart that one can see rightly; what is essential is invisible to the eye."

Notes

1. Anonymous, "The King's Great Gift," in Jack Canfield and Jacqueline Miller, *Heart at Work: Stories and Strategies for Building Self-Esteem and Reawakening the Soul at Work* (New York: McGraw-Hill, 1996), 186.

2. Dalai Lama quoted in Frances Vaughan, "Spiritual Issues in Psychotherapy," *The Journal of Transpersonal Psychology* 23, no. 2 (1991): 118–119.

3. Scriptures from Charles R. Swindoll, *Improving Your Serve: The Art of Unselfish Living* (Waco, Texas: Word Books, 1981), 119.

4. O. P. Ghai, compiler and editor, *Thoughts of the World's Great Religions: A Guide to the Understanding of the Fundamental Unity Underlying the Twelve Great Living Religions of the World* (Pinellas Park, Florida: Top of the Mountain Publishing, 1995), 100–101.

5. Ibid.

6. Wayne Muller, *How, Then, Shall We Live?* (New York: Bantam, 1996), 207.

7. Adapted from Roy H. Schaefer, "The Stewardship of Appropriate Ministry," *Saints Herald* 126, no. 3 (February 1, 1979): 59–60.

8. Roland G. Anderson, "Love and Service—Zion," *Saints Herald* 125, no. 11 (November 1978): 686.

9. Sheldon Kopp, *All God's Children Are Lost, but Only a Few Can Play the Piano: Finding a Life That Is Truly Your Own* (New York: Prentice Hall, 1991), 99.

10. Marilyn vos Savant, *Of Course I'm for Monogamy: I'm Also for Everlasting Peace and an End to Taxes* (New York: St. Martin's Press, 1996), 27.

11. Irv Fulman in Kathy Collard Miller and D. Larry Miller, *God's Vitamin "C" for the Spirit* (Lancaster, Pennsylvania: Starburst Publications, 1996), 274.

Chapter 4

The Elder as Presider

Paul M. Edwards

Though most elders will find themselves presiding a great deal, it is not a well-understood function. To "be in charge" is both a responsibility and an opportunity that, for the good of all concerned, needs to encompass more than announcing the hymns. Certainly, the calling of this priesthood office is larger than this particular function, but true presiding is a significant function in itself.

The elder is often called on to preside, almost automatically, not only in services of worship, but also in business meetings and even less formal gatherings of church members. The laws of the church, enhanced by tradition, assume that even if others are assigned the duties of directing a service, any elder present still retains the primary responsibility. That is, they sometimes preside only by their very presence. On most occasions, the assignment to preside has somehow been transformed into the job of directing or performing. It is seen both as a job to be done—usually after someone else has detailed how it is to be done—or a chance to guide or direct the work of others.

The term "preside" means literally to sit before—in front of—others, to provide management or control. It is used in the Restoration to mean leader, or manager, of a service or a group. But the word describes a further dimension from either leadership or management because it has acquired other meanings—traditional meanings—as well.

As we take a look at the calling to the office of elder, it is wise to focus briefly on the responsibilities of the presider and to look at some of the more significant aspects of this calling.

To Pre-live

One way to define the word "presider" is to point out that it means "to go before, to pre-live." To "pre-live," as we are looking at it, involves two important things. It first means bringing experience to bear upon a situation. The presider is the specialist who brings to his or her role the experience of previous encounters with time-tested methods, with uniformity and concern, knowing how to move and adjust to get the most from the activity and to meet the needs of the people. For the experienced presider, there are no great surprises, no panic, no loss of focus.

True, the elder must start somewhere getting this experience and is not automatically skilled. But the calling to preside reflects both the potential and the expression of understandings and skills that come into use at this time.

The second understanding of "pre-living" lies in the concept of going before, anticipating the results, or looking, feeling, and discerning what such a service or meeting will accomplish. Thus one prepares ahead of time—going into the journey of spiritual seeking and response ahead of those in the congregation—and sensing the power of the ending as one prepares the beginning.

To pre-live the event is to approach the role in anticipation of the future, to see within the not-yet and experience the growth and celebration resident there. The presider celebrates what is being sought rather than relying too much on the nostalgia of that which is past, or on becoming too dependent on maintaining the status quo.

Credibility

Another aspect of the role of the presider is to provide legitimacy to what is happening. That is, the role of the presider—whether he or she is sitting behind the podium or on the next to the last row—is to lend to the service the credibility of an honest presentation: to be the church in this moment of gathering.

The necessity of this, as well as the difficulty in accomplishing this, lies in the fact that we live in a world in which presentation is often more important than content. Today, the primary concern appears to be in the cosmetic rather than in addressing life's realities. Our society, at least in the Western world, has become enamored with appearing important, putting on a good face, and making things look good. It is a fantasy at which we work diligently.

Think for a moment how many people in this generation make their living telling lies; that is, misrepresenting reality as even they know it. Without pointing any fingers—for few of us are without guilt—consider how many untruths are told in one day by employers, advertisers, and newscasters on television, by salespersons and agents and, on an even more sophisticated level, by organizations and corporations whose purpose is to tap into one's resources rather than to provide a service.

Recently, as I was thinking through a talk I was to give about "Lying in America," I decided to count the number of times I knew I was lied to in a given day. It began with the waitress who, when I asked for "real" coffee, informed me it was in the pot with the green top. Then, carrying the same pot, she informed the lady in the next booth that the pot with the green top contained decaffeinated coffee. Of minor significance? Probably, but it reflects the concerns I have. We have found it easier to misrepresent reality than to deal with it. The real concern is, of course, that people build their lives on a reality that will not support their decisions.

To follow the illustration, the role of the manager is to preside over the restaurant. It is his or her responsibility to see that what the restaurant represents is reality—that the coffee is what I ask for, that the conditions are sanitary, that I am reasonably charged. If I have no faith in the manager, I have none in the restaurant. While this illustration, like all illustrations, fails if pushed too far, my point is that the presider is the one who vouches for the integrity of the action.

When I am led through the phases of worship, I do so in full anticipation that those in charge will conduct themselves with integrity and honesty. I trust that they will insist on the integrity of those involved. I anticipate that what is done is done in good faith, and that I am not being "sold a bill of goods," lied to, or led to believe others are concerned when they are not.

Obviously, this does not mean that I expect the presider to agree with everything done or said, but rather that his or her presence testifies that what is being done or said reflects the best beliefs and most honest response from those with responsibility.

I seek from the presider not so much order, or the flawless flow of functions, but leadership. That leadership may well reflect a position that pulls and stretches me, but not one that misleads me.

Leadership or Management?

Closely related to this function, and one that reflects the great paradox of religious leadership, is the balance between the new and the old. For the leader is called to lead, and very often that means addressing the new: pushing growth and seeking alternative expression. At the same time, it is to the leaders of the faith that we turn for assurance and hope and to whom we look for the preservation of the best that is in us.

Thus the presider walks the thin line between leadership and management. The leader is a mover and shaker, a maker of things happening, an innovator, insightful and often unpredictable, full of understandings and conceptions that delight and surprise us and that will, at the same time, bring discomfort to our enemies and often make the lives of the jurisdictional officers less than comfortable.

Yet, there are some aspects of the presider's role that would be identified as manager. Managers, paradoxically, are those who reflect more predictability, are more inclined to conform to the existing ways of doing things, and act as team players who are dedicated not only to the group but to the overall organization.

By rights we have some reason to expect our presider to be reflective of the larger organization, not to step too far outside the prevailing understanding so as to defeat the purpose of the gathering. We often expect our presiders to be more conservative and predictable in their roles than we wish to be in ours.

Balanced thus, the presider carries the unique responsibility of being the innovator and preserver of the tradition, the delightful change agent yet predictable guide, the unique individualist who is a team player, always working to divide the right from the practical, the good from the convenient, the individual from the group.

Thus the presider must be aware of the need to balance group expectations against personal uniqueness and desire; to confirm and lift up the individual; to care without rumor or an invasion of rights; to balance the line between convictions and advocacy.

Balancing the Secular and the Sacred

Another aspect of the role of the presider is to serve as the connection—as well as the transition—between the world in which we all function and the church to which we have gathered. The presider closes the gap and decreases the diversity between sacred and secular. The "call to worship" is not only a reading or a scriptural reference, it is the drawing together of those gathered into the presence of potential, and it eases the congregation—individually and as a group—into the spirit of worship.

To do this, of course, requires that we make of the service a secular as well as a sacred event by bringing the sacred and the secular closer into unity. The significance here is to overcome the normal tendency to divide our lives: living the secular all week long and retreating into the sacred only on Sunday morning. In so doing, we deny the holistic nature of God's world, assuming that some aspects of that world are lacking, or without, the creative influence. It is to the presider that we turn for aid in bringing God into our everyday world through the unity of worship.

Integration

The presider's role also involves the capacity for integration: to see the wholeness, yet recognizing all the parts as well as the whole. While most congregations tend to see themselves as the center of the church world, and this is understandable, it is the role of presider to inject the larger worldview into that which is done: to remind the worshipers of their larger calling as God's people in a larger world, to see beyond the horizons of their own values, and to be a part of the interrelatedness of the world at large.

Though it is much better, there is still a tendency to separate parts of the service as if chores to be done: call to worship, prayers (beginning and ending), the Word, the bishop's request. But to be really meaningful, the service must reflect the reality that each of our expressions of worship are significant and that it is in commingling these activities that we celebrate, rather than memorialize, the events of our lives.

Enhance the Effectiveness of Others

The presider has the responsibility to make others effective. That is, she or he provides them with what they need to be as effective as they can be—to worship, to praise, to beseech, to lead, to reflect, to articulate that which is within them. It is perhaps unnecessary to say, maybe even redundant, that one of the most significant roles of the presider is to facilitate the service. It is so necessary to avoid the "same old business" approach to a service. It is more necessary than we sometimes imagine to seek out those who are there to help us.

Over the last fifteen years, I have traveled a great deal among the congregations of the church. I have always been kindly and graciously received. But I also have a list of horror stories about ineffective presiders—that is, individuals who did not understand they needed to help me in ministering in their locales. The presider must not expect everyone who takes part to know the local customs, to acknowledge immediate needs, or to be aware of special problems. Sometimes the procedures need to be rehearsed for the sake of those not so aware—policies long held but never revealed, or perhaps to tell the speaker what you as presider intend to do, when they are to speak, how long they should talk, and if they will be introduced.

The presider must seek to make it easy for everyone else in the service, or meeting, to concentrate on their contribution. Far better to be thinking of what it is we want to say about the love of God than worrying about when we are supposed to speak, or if we will be introduced, or what the message really was behind the humorous reference to the fact people get up and go home after forty-five minutes of church.

Compassion

A key ingredient in the makeup of the presider is compassion. The one who will preside must be willing to stand beside the sufferer, to bear the pain of the wounded, and to acknowledge the difficulty of focus when your world is ill at ease. It means to proceed with an inner integrity that acknowledges the plight of the individual as well as the needs of the congregation as a whole, to relate what is happening in the worship service to the inner world where people live, as well as to seek to bring each heart from within and refresh it on the altar of combined love.

To be a presider is to be the wounded healer, avoiding self-righteousness and judgment. But at the same time it means to be fully aware of your own agenda, your own needs, and what this says to those who come to worship. Such a knowledge requires the willingness to know yourself, to avoid the tendency to self-deception, and to enlarge the capacity for self-awareness and consciousness.

Hope and Promise

This may sound like a lot, and that it is pushing the role of the presider to be all inclusive. Perhaps it *is* requiring a great deal. But remember, when you sit before, or pre-live, for those who are your followers for the time, you are their leader: the image of their hope and the promise of their safekeeping. That is a calling for the most concerned of elders.

Chapter 5

The Elder as Steward

Barbara L. Carter

Introduction

I remember the feelings of anger and frustration as my father and I were heading home from church one Christmas Sunday. We had just finished our special service attended by the additional people who came to church only on holidays, such as Christmas and Easter. I turned to my father, who had been the pastor and only priesthood member for as long as I could remember, and vented my frustration. "Why don't you tell them they need to come to church more than two times a year?" I cried. "Don't you just want to scream, *hypocrites* to them? Doesn't it bother you that they don't support you and the congregation during the rest of the year?" There was a brief moment of silence. Then Dad responded in the truest sense of being a steward, "I am happy that they come to church when they do, because it is then that they have a chance to hear the message of Jesus Christ."

I am reminded of this interaction with my father on a yearly basis, every Christmas service. Over the years, it has become a warm memory because of the example it set for me. As an elder, my father believed it was his responsibility to have a place ready for people to encounter Christ and then nurture them as they grew. He was neither judgmental nor condemning, just ready.

Elders are the stewards of the stewards. They are commissioned to care for and nurture the people as they grow in their response to the ministry of Jesus Christ, their personal stewardship. "Stewardship is a process activity by which God is honored as Creator and humans try with diligence and consecration to use the things of this world in such a way that the places where they live may shine as Zion, the redeemed of the Lord."[1] It is the process of developing into full maturation the potentials within each person as they live and recognize their place and importance in the world community.

In the scriptures stewards are portrayed as those responsible for another's possessions or assets. They are given the responsibility to act on behalf of the owner. The image of a steward being the manager of land and crops is one that is in the forefront of our thoughts when we think about the examples provided for us. What is produced by the land (the quantity and quality) is directly dependent on the thoughts and actions of the steward.

The elders' role of steward is like that of one who cares for the land and crops, only their work is done in the lives of individuals and congregations. This is done through exercising the gifts and skills they have developed and offering them back to God in service. Just as a steward over land prepares the soil for the chosen crop, the elders prepare the body of Christ for the greatest possible receptivity to God's grace and love. This is accomplished by establishing relationships with the people, becoming involved in their lives, knowing their hopes and fears, and encouraging their journey with Christ. When the elders know and love the people, they can best discern the type of leadership that is needed. With the direction of the Holy Spirit, spiritual guidance is provided to God's people.

Continuing with this analogy, the role of the elder as a steward can be viewed as four areas of emphasis: preparation, planting, nurturing, and harvesting.

The Preparation

Just as the farmer spends time evaluating the climate, soil, and growing season before choosing a crop, elders spend time responding to the ministry of Christ by investing themselves in the lives of the people in the congregation and their neighbors and friends. As they come to know people, they can develop the type of relationship that allows the elder to be aware of the ministry needed in their lives. This preparation by the elder is vital to meeting the needs of people. If farmers were to plant a crop because it was their favorite or because it was the one they knew how to grow, without considering climate, soil, and growing season, it is possible that the farmers would not have any crop to harvest. If allowed, the Holy Spirit will push us out of what is known and comfortable and into areas where spiritual growth and new vision become realities in the lives of people.

This preparation time is preparing the elders, as well, for possible service. By taking stock of their strengths and weaknesses, the elders can be actively engaged in activities that will enhance their ministry and strengthen their relationship with their creator. They can develop relationships with others who have different skills allowing people whose ministry complements each other to work together. The elder does not stand alone in priesthood but pulls all elements together in preparation for servanthood.

The elders are to administer in spiritual things (Doctrine and Covenants 104:7) and hold the keys of the spiritual blessings (Doctrine and Covenants 104:9a). There is great responsibility for them to be fully prepared, so they can accomplish the intent of their calling. As a steward of the stewards, there is also great responsibility in seeing that others have made their own preparation for service.

Just as we are involved in our own preparation, God is also at work preparing people to welcome the presence of God back into their lives. "My Spirit is reaching out to numerous souls even now and there are many who will respond if you, my people, will bear affirmative testimony of my love and my desires for all to come unto me" (Doctrine and Covenants 153:9b).

The Planting

"The purpose of priesthood is to bear witness of the love of God and of the saving grace and sacrifice of Jesus Christ."[2] This is planting the seed. Elders are called to lead by example, in all areas, but especially by being ready to give a positive witness at any time. Because one never knows what others hear or remember, the "faith and godly character of members of the Melchisedec priesthood should be evidenced by an affirmative and cheerful heart and countenance, and cleanliness of spirit, body, and clothing."[3] The elders have to make a conscious decision: What type of crop will be planted? The elders' response to this question is their response to knowing Jesus Christ. It is their stewardship.

The elders set an example in all areas of spiritual and temporal matters. As elders strive to lead a life in service and in accord with the spirit of the law, they are blessed. These blessings are not just for the elders themselves. They are for the people around them as well. When one is blessed by the grace of God, all are blessed. As a community of stewards, we share in all things, both spiritual and temporal.

Elders also help others to be ready to share their experiences of how God is working in their lives. People are given opportunities to learn how to verbalize their experiences with their creator. This is often hard, and it takes work to articulate moving experiences with our limited vocabulary. People are encouraged and challenged to ready themselves and then begin sharing. Sharing our verbal testimony is one way of witnessing. It is one that we all must be a part of. Yet there are other ways of planting seeds of God's love and grace in peoples' lives. Learning to love people, unconditionally, without reservation, and investing yourself in their lives, reflects your relationship to the Creator. Being involved in activities that promote peace and justice plants seeds of God's grace and love. These seeds need care and nurture.

The Nurturing

When seeds are planted, farmers do not leave the field and take a cruise to the Caribbean hoping the seed will develop and mature and be ready to harvest when the farmer returns. Farmers walk the land examining the plants and looking for weeds and disease that may have infested their crop. They give the plants more food when they need it and ensure that not too much food is given at certain times. The moisture level in the soil is kept at optimal levels so that the harvest will be its best. Farmers cultivate their fields, and they get rid of the weeds, removing anything that may weaken or contaminate the crop. This makes the plants stronger and the yield greater. This is the process of nurturing.

Elders who are participating in their call as stewards are always nurturing. They need to ensure that the body stays spiritually healthy by providing spiritual food when needed. They walk among the people ready to uplift and encourage. They are involved in keeping the vision alive in their hearts. People of all ages need support and love along their spiritual journeys. The need for someone to be there is vital when those people are immersed with others who are seeking a life with God.

Nurturing has many aspects. It can be as simple as saying a prayer or as complex as being a constant companion for a person in pain. It takes place in church school classes, prayer meetings, youth group activities, and in everyday phone calls. It is accomplished in quiet moments of reflection and in jubilant activities of celebration.

Nurturing is always gentle, with love, for the purpose of making people stronger. It is not permission to condemn or chastise, even out of concern. We sometimes feel that we need to point out to someone what he or she is doing wrong. I believe a good steward helps people turn their focus in a different direction. This is done by being an example of living in light and by slowly and painstakingly sharing bits and pieces of that light. If you have a plant that is leaning awkwardly in one direction, almost ready to fall over, you don't push it back in one fell swoop. You gently apply pressure, and you turn it so it will grow toward the light. Nurturing helps people become stronger by their own actions and growth, not by someone else holding them up.

The Harvesting

When a plant has been nurtured into full maturation, it is ready to be harvested. As a community of believers, our journey does not end with our individual spiritual growth but pulls us into the consecration of servanthood. The harvest is offering who and what we are to the service of God.

Elders are called to look for and see the skills and gifts that are evident in people and then lead them into a firstfruits lifestyle. The elders are stewards who encourage us to use our gifts to enhance the life of the congregation and the church as a whole.

Each gift is vital. If it is left untapped, it will soon be unavailable to the body. It is just like a crop: if not harvested, it will die on the plant; but when harvested, it continues to provide value. If a grain is left on the plant in rice farming, it will drop into the soil and may come back the next year as a plant. Great! you might say. But these rice plants are called "red rice," and they devalue the crop. After plants are nurtured and matured, they need to be used. Elders are responsible for managing the harvest and using it to its fullest potential. Just as the farmer finds the best market for the crop, elders search to find the best way possible to engage people in the mission of the church. In the Doctrine and Covenants we are reminded that all are called: "therefore, if ye have desires to serve God, ye are called to the work, for, behold the field is white already to harvest" (Doctrine and Covenants 4:1c).

The elders as stewards are accountable for their own response to the ministry of Jesus Christ. They are also accountable for those in their congregations and those with whom they meet. It is a burden to carry; it is a great joy to participate. "And this is my glory, that perhaps I may be an instrument in the hands of God to bring some soul to repentance; and this is my joy" (Alma 15:61).

Conclusion

All are called to witness. All are called to be stewards. All are called to prepare their lives for service to God and humankind. All are called to minister, to plant, to nurture, and to harvest. The elder as a steward is called to serve those who respond to the call as well as those who have yet to hear.

Being a steward is responding to the ministry of Jesus Christ as love, hope, joy, and peace permeate your soul and you know with assurance that God loves you. "We are to grow in the likeness of Christ and become one with him as the powerful, moving force of love is expressed in the giving of mind, body, spiritual, and material means for the coming kingdom."[4]

Notes

1. The Presiding Bishopric, *Stand in Holy Places*, from *Family Financial Planning: The ForGiving Heart* (Independence, Missouri: Herald House, 1992), 39–40.
2. Clifford A. Cole and Richard A. Brown, compilers, *The Priesthood Manual* (Independence, Missouri: Herald House, 1990), 17.
3. Ibid., 61.
4. *Stand in Holy Places*, 58.

Chapter 6

Elder: *Imagi*Vision

Jerry W. Nieft

Introduction

Who is an elder? Is an elder a person or an office, a way of being or a job to be done? Should an elder have "vision"? What is there to see other than the obvious things that need to be done? Is an elder's vision a gift or a work? How is it realized?

In early church founding experiences, elders are described as priesthood leaders who are to be ordained according to the "gifts and callings of God" to them by the power of the Holy Ghost. They take the lead in meetings, teach, exhort, expound, baptize, confirm, lay on hands, act as standing ministers, do missionary work, and so on. Beyond all the tasks in the office description of the elder is the implicit understanding that elders have a depth of spiritual experience and commitment that enables them to lead the church according to the guidance of the Spirit. How is guidance experienced and how can it be translated into a compelling vision that inspires and motivates the church to fulfill its calling to be the body of Christ serving in the world?

When leaders realize a need for new direction and vision, they often quote the ancient wisdom of Proverbs 29:18, "Where there is no vision, the people perish...." While the proverb is true and appropriate, it is cast in a negative and minimal way. If it were recast, what would be its affirmation and impact? "Where there is vision, the people ... exist? ... move forward? ... grow? ... break through? ... prosper?"

If the general direction and tenor of recorded history and prehistory are any indication of what is emerging in creation and humanity, then vision and leading are certainly about more than just "not perishing" or "getting by." Leading with vision is about helping people and their communities experience breakthroughs in living maximally, with increase occurring both through gradual evolution and surprising quantum leaps of grace. Leaders with vision participate with God in nothing less than the unfolding of life and order in God's expanding creation.

Jesus had such a compelling vision and lived it as is required of any good leader. He announced that he came to give abundant life and that everyone must repent, for the kingdom of God was at hand. The word "repent" comes from the Greek word *metanoia*, which means to know differently, to have a change of mind, to have a shift in consciousness. If one repents, one sees everything differently, with new vision. The vision is that the kingdom is near, at hand, surprisingly available—not at a distance or delayed by time—but as close as a new way of seeing and knowing. It is certainly good news that the vision is accessible to anyone open to repentance.

Jesus identified himself variously in the "I am's" of the Gospel according to John as the way, the truth, the life, the living water, the bread of life, the gate, the light, and the resurrection. The vision Jesus followed produced an identity in him that was transformative, healing, and saving for himself and others who were willing to share it with him. His metaphoric identities revealed through symbol the internal life strategies or "Christ consciousness" that he lived and expressed externally in his ministry. The vision he saw and appropriated into his being was nourishing and refreshing like bread and living water, revealing and penetrating like light, directing and guiding like a path, and transmuting and transducing like resurrection. Paul's assessment of what Jesus did informed his counsel to the Philippian saints for their vision:

> Let the same mind be in you that was in Christ Jesus, who, though he was in the form of God, did not regard equality with God as something to be exploited, but emptied himself, taking the form of a [servant], being born in human likeness. And being found in human form, he humbled himself and became obedient to the point of death—even death on a cross.—Philippians 2:5–8 NRSV

How can elders in the Church of Jesus Christ empty themselves and be filled with a vision for life that is congruent with the Christ-consciousness of Jesus and comprehensible to the people of today and tomorrow?

Seeing Life Anew

There have been many rational programs and techniques devised over the years to help individuals and organizations develop a vision for the future. These approaches are certainly beneficial and make deliberate and concrete what can otherwise be vague and unconsidered. Vision and mission statements are useful in approaching life from a proactive rather than a reactive stance. Such methods, however, rely on verbal, analytical thinking that sees the world in a very narrow, limited, fragmented, sequential, linear way—the main talent of the left hemisphere of the brain. The result is "vision" that manages more effectively and efficiently the same or similar view of reality. At best, it is incremental change for the better. It is no substitute, however, for an exciting, fundamental change of global perspective that is the talent of the right hemisphere of the brain. Effective management must not be confused with visionary leadership. One *manages* from left-hemisphere talents of verbal and mathematical analysis, but one *leads* from the right-hemisphere talent of global, holistic, transrational vision.

Elders seeking vision must first look beyond doing more elder's tasks well in whatever program might be current. Having vision is more about learning "to be" in a different way rather than doing more in the same way. "Being" is an internal experience with existence that defines everything else to which one relates. To be different and visionary is to see beyond the illusions of the typical world frame most people use. To use a computer metaphor, it is choosing different perceptual software settings than the "default" settings popular culture mandates. How does the elder start to lay aside illusions and "get real" by appropriating a more authentic vision of the way the world operates?

Margaret Wheatley is an organization and management theorist who believes that vision must proceed from an understanding of what the world is really like. To misunderstand the world and how it operates is to start from premises that will distort and sabotage any vision derived from them. Most current visions operating in human culture are based on antiquated science that no longer adequately informs modern thought, excites the imagination, or ministers to the needs of the human soul. In a recent article titled "The Unplanned Organization,"[1] Margaret Wheatley lists a number of affirmations about the world that are suggested by current scientific evidence and theory but not necessarily appreciated and utilized by our culture. The assertions have profound implications for how and what we envision. How do they instruct our vision for the ministry of the elder in the world today?

- We live in a world in which life wants to happen.
- Organizations are living systems, or at least the people in them are living systems.
- We live in a universe that is alive, creative, and experimenting all the time to discover what's possible.

- It is the natural tendency of life to organize—to seek greater levels of complexity and diversity.
- Life uses messes to get to well-ordered solutions.
- Life is intent on finding what works, not what's right.
- Life creates more possibilities as it engages with opportunities.
- Life organizes around identity.[2]

These affirmations inform our visioning in several important ways. The universe is alive and constantly experimenting with potentiality and actuality. It used to be fashionable to cite the second law of thermodynamics and point out rather pessimistically that the universe is like a machine that will eventually run out of usable energy. Such a view did not take into account the contribution of living systems. Instead of everything winding down into disorder and chaos, the universe is also actually organizing into more complex and diverse forms through living systems. Rather than committing suicide, the universe appears to be pursuing purpose and meaning as it organizes around identity. The universe is self-organizing. Wheatley says,

> Life organizes spontaneously and creatively, but it organizes around a self. It is making self. For me, this feels like further evidence that consciousness is at work in everything because you can't organize around a self without being conscious that you are a self. So when we see self-organization, I believe what we're watching is consciousness forming itself into different identifiable beings. Thus, we live in a world which is truly co-creative, in which you and I cannot exist in isolation.[3]

Instead of a bleak scenario of scarcity, adversarialism, and purposelessness, which has characterized the paradigm of reality that currently is being challenged, the scientific evidence of the new physics suggests just the contrary. Something or someone wants things to go in a direction opposite to chaos and beat death. Order and purpose and life "buck" the odds and happen anyway. There is an entelechy,[4] or drive, to actualize from all the possibilities and potentials available at any given moment what we as elders in the Church of Jesus Christ would call God's creative will. This is the same basic affirmation that God gave to Moses when asked about how things work and come to be:

> And worlds without number have I created, and I also created them for mine own purpose; and by the Son I created them, which is mine Only Begotten.... And the Lord God spake unto Moses, saying, The heavens, they are many and they can not be numbered unto man, but they are numbered unto me, for they are mine; and as one earth shall pass away, and the heavens thereof, even so shall another come; and there is no end to my works, neither to my words; for this is my work and my glory, to bring to pass the immortality, and eternal life of man.
>
> —Doctrine and Covenants 22:21c, 23a–b

Even though there is a teleological[5] drive tending to lead the universe into higher expressions of life and identity, there is no set pattern or template that determines outcomes. The future is open and pregnant with ever-expanding possibilities. The physics called quantum mechanics asserts that we affect the real world by the way we choose to observe it, the so-called observer effect. We participate in the possibilities of the moment and thereby collapse one of them into a particular actuality by the way we think, choose, and observe. The implications are astounding. Conscious awareness and observation actually help create reality moment by moment. Individual human thought and choice really matter in the scheme of things. Every observation, thought, and choice of everyone impacts the whole. What each person envisions contributes to the possible outcomes of each moment.

If quantum mechanics, which has already served well for almost a century, turns out to be a faithful, durable model for reality, then human vision and choice must be acknowledged as extremely important and critical factors in the way the future unfolds. The way we see the world has profound consequences. The future is open, but it is determined by the observation and participation of conscious beings. God, and those created in God's image, together "see" reality into being.

The way the future may be left "to chance" is by everyone abdicating responsibility for deliberately and intentionally envisioning it—just let it happen. On the other hand, if many develop consensus visions in the direction of what they discern to be the will of God, then the probability for the future unfolding in ways congruent with God's will increases. In effect, humanity can choose to participate in or oppose that general bias and drive toward life, complexity, diversity, and possibility that is God's will for creation.

The universe is very much under construction. There is purpose or design that wants to elicit consciousness and self, but the blueprints are fluid. We, with God, are architects, contractors, and craftpersons cocreating what is potential into what is actual or real. Elders are no different from anyone else in terms of access to vision or realization of it through participation. Elders, as representatives of Jesus Christ, however, have committed to assist and lead others who want to capture and help realize the unfolding vision, too. Elders in the Church of Jesus Christ are charged with the responsibility and privilege of taking the lead in helping the church and the world envision the future as it is wanting to unfold—an expression of the combined participation of conscious selves with God, the emerging kingdom of God.

The Church of Jesus Christ is being called to imagine the future with God. The past is important; it is benchmark, reference, tradition, and memory. The present is critical, for its instantaneous moments are the venue of life and realization of potential. The future is open to authentic, genuine imagining with God. To imagine is to image in acute visual detail in conscious awareness what is potential. It is an additional creation of future possibility that informs and awaits the present. Whether our imaginings are realized depends on our choosing and observing moment by moment. If God's work and glory is the immortality and eternal life of humanity, then we are challenged by God to imagine it so through our response moment by moment to what we discern to be the prompting of the Spirit. If God is love as John testifies, then God is *for* us, not against us. We are challenged to imagine it so and behave it into being in the flow of present moments. Recently the church has again been challenged to imagine the future, a particular quality of future with God:

> Lift up your eyes and fix them on *the place beyond the horizon* to which you are sent. Journey in trust, assured that the great and marvelous work is *for this time and for all time.*
> ...Be faithful to the spirit of the Restoration, mindful that it is a spirit of *adventure*, openness, and searching.
> ...Embrace the blessing of your many differences. Be reminded once again that *the gifts of all are necessary in order that divine purposes may be accomplished....*
> Be courageous and visionary, *believing in the power of just a few vibrant witnesses to transform the world.*[6] (emphasis added)

The calling to be a disciple of Jesus Christ and lead others with vision as an elder representing Jesus Christ is certainly daunting. Margaret Mead once pointed out that the power of a few people to get great things accomplished should never be doubted, for indeed that is how most significant change has historically occurred. The conscious awareness and intervention of good people cannot only forestall evil but transform the world for good.

Realizing the Vision

The pursuing, recognizing, and realizing of an unfolding vision is accomplished more by surrender than brute force. It is a grace that one participates in rather than forces to happen. The vision that opens up is more than *a* vision, if it is genuine. It is *the* vision appropriate for a person's participation in the whole. It is at least a unique part or subset of the vision God wants to unfold in the universe, if there is indeed such a thing as a part distinguishable from the whole.

Joseph Jaworski's new book, *Synchronicity: The Inner Path of Leadership,*[7] is a practical guide and testimony of how a person perceives his or her particular vision and pursues it to accomplish life's purpose. Jaworski explains the surprising insights he has acquired through telling the story of his life. He experienced, in the midst of a successful career as a lawyer and businessman, a disturbing urge or call to do something entirely different with his life. He was afraid to consider it. As the large and small events of life continued to impact him, Jaworski's conscious awareness of life and its principles began to expand and suggest further that he was being called to accomplish something beyond himself, something for the world. He *felt* and came to believe he was to create an international institute and program for developing capable future leaders of the world. The desire welling up within his being was insistent, and he finally gave in to it. He surrendered to the entelechy or force inviting him into an unimagined future. He literally quit his old life of security and started a new life based on faith, without knowing what the next step would be or whether it would succeed.

Once Jaworski committed unequivocally and unreservedly to the vision growing in his awareness, he experienced to his surprise a "flow" of events, people, and resources that came together providentially to help realize it. He founded the American Leadership Forum in 1980. He has continued to follow the leadings of the unfolding vision in his life. Now he works for the MIT Center for Organizational Learning and has helped create the Centre for Generative Leadership. His response to the emergent vision in his life is making a difference in the leaders the world has to offer; they, in turn, will help shape the future in more competent, principled ways.

Everyone, like Jaworski, is called to a unique vision and contribution to the whole of life. Elders are. The people to whom elders minister are. Although there is a dynamic operating that desires everyone to participate in the unfolding future of life, the vision and the path are not obvious nor is the way necessarily easy. Elders in the Church of Jesus Christ are ordained according to the gifts and callings of God unto them. They lead with spiritual depth and insight. They wrestle with life issues and pursue the leadings of the Spirit in their own lives. They then draw on their life's experience in serving with others who are going through similar challenges. Elders serve others as they themselves are served by life.

There are several important understandings Jaworski experienced that helped him focus and realize the vision that entered his awareness. They are somewhat mystical, and following them produces a life experience Joseph Campbell described as the "hero's journey," an archetype that depicts the change process in individuals.[8] The journey has several components. There is a preparing for the journey in which one feels dissatisfied with life as it is. A vague call or restlessness is perceived. At some point a decision is made to "cross the threshold" and go on the quest.

With this decision comes the experience of people, events, and resources appearing at just the right place and time to nurture and advance the quest. Such happenings are synchronicities, a term and principle originally used by Carl Jung to describe the meaningful coincidence of two or more things not related by causal chains. They are evidence that the universe is encouraging the quest and wanting the hero or heroine to see the next part of the vision. The journey continues with many trials that test commitment to the vision. There are successes and failures. Both are opportunities for learning, for embracing, and for letting go. Finally, the quest yields the gift of transformation and renewal.

The hero's journey is an archetype of everyone's journey through life. It is about perceiving and pursuing a destiny that gradually matures into awareness. The quest to realize the vision transforms the person along the way. Examples are Homer's Odysseus, the life and ministry of Jesus Christ, and the life and ministry of each disciple of Jesus Christ. Jaworski discovered tenets that helped him in his quest from vision to gift that have remarkable similarities to those already cited by Wheatley and suggested by modern science.

1. It is important for us to learn that being is more important than doing. Often we try to manipulate life and make it happen. It is ultimately more satisfying and rewarding to cooperate with it and allow it to flow through us in its teleological drive to create higher expressions of self.

2. It is important to be open to knowing from a completely new perspective, a *metanoia* or repentance. Life is more than we suspect. We can participate in the unfolding and imagining of it.

3. The journey reveals that we are not alone or separate. We are together with others and everything. The universe is relational. We matter. Everything does. All are one, an interconnected whole.

4. We erect artificial boundaries in our living that we must learn to dissolve or transcend. Love softens and expands boundaries to include more and more, so that the illusion of parts is replaced with the reality of the whole.

5. Heroes and heroines learn that others are authentic human beings, too. As visionary leaders they inspire others to be all that they can be.

6. Total commitment to the call is the key factor that facilitates and advances the quest. Synchronicities appear and nurture the vision to completion.

7. Commitment is twofold. It requires taking action, but it also necessitates a shift in consciousness, a different way of being, a *metanoia*. Tak-

ing action with the same mindset just produces more of the same. When we are transformed, our commitment takes on a new, more powerful, effective nature. We discern the world with new vision and use it to put forth each new step on the path as it is revealed, moment by moment. Our commitment takes us on the heroic journey to become what we are called to be.[9]

Seeing in a Mirror Dimly

For we know only in part, and we prophesy only in part; but when the complete comes, the partial will come to an end. When I was a child, I spoke like a child, I thought like a child, I reasoned like a child; when I became an adult, I put an end to childish ways. For now we see in a mirror dimly, but then we will see face to face. Now I only know in part; then I will know fully, even as I have been fully known. And now faith, hope, and love abide, these three; and the greatest of these is love.—I Corinthians 13:9–13, NRSV

Paul understood the importance of vision and realized the limitations and imperfections of human discernment. He was confident that things would continue to clear up as we pursue vision with authentic interest and discipline. The vision is to see things as they truly are, to know and understand perfectly, which ultimately means to love each other face to face.

Although it does not yet appear what we may ultimately be, we know the vision Jesus Christ calls us to is centered at its core in love. It calls us to recognize the infinite worth of each human being. It calls us to care for all aspects of creation. It calls us to realize that the universe is relational. We matter, and it matters how we live. Our individual and collective visions are crucial to the unfolding of life's purpose in the universe.

There are a number of probabilities and potentialities maturing for expression in the twenty-first century. Whether they are realized depends on our vision and participation. The emerging vision may have some of the following characteristics:

1. There will be a continued exploration of spirituality. People will pursue spiritual disciplines and expand their appreciation for the quality of the "inner" experience. There will be more emphasis on inside-out rather than outside-in strategies.

2. There will be increased emphasis on building real community and authentic human relationships. There will be a coming together to counter the separating that has been occurring for several generations as governmental, economic, and social decisions have been made using old paradigms that are increasingly dysfunctional.

3. Religion and science will come together and inform one another. There will be more integration of knowing with less artificial separation into noncommunicating or hostile disciplines.

4. While transportation and communication and computerization will create life that is globally informed and interconnected, it will be increasingly important to live a high quality of life locally.

It does not yet appear what the twenty-first century will ultimately be. Nor does anyone know what the church will be or how ministry will occur. There are vague outlines coming into view. The challenge is for all, and leaders in particular, to envision the future with God. It is our opportunity to be cocreators of the kingdom of God. It is near at hand.

Notes

1. Margaret Wheatley, "The Unplanned Organization," *Noetic Sciences Review* 37 (Spring 1996): 16–23.
2. Ibid., 18–19.
3. Ibid., 20.
4. Entelechy, meaning actuality or the press toward actuality, as distinguished from potentiality.
5. Teleology means directed toward a definite end or ultimate purpose.
6. W. Grant McMurray, "Words of Counsel to the Church," *Saints Herald* 143, no. 6 (June 1996): 228.
7. Joseph Jaworski, *Synchronicity: The Inner Path of Leadership* (San Francisco: Berrett-Koehler, 1996).
8. Joseph Campbell, *The Hero with a Thousand Faces* (Princeton, New Jersey: Princeton University Press, 1949).
9. Jaworski, 69.

Chapter 7

The Office and Mission

Shelby M. Barnes

Some years ago Jacques Barzun wrote a wonderful book called *The Culture We Deserve* (Middletown, Connecticut: Wesleyan University Press, 1989). Barzun, a longtime observer and literary interpreter of American society, warned that once again the world was suffering from getting too much of what it wanted. Modern people have asked for the moon, and have pretty much gotten it all, and they are now overwhelmed with their successes. But the question of meaning has grown louder. Why has all this not brought us the peace, hope, acceptance, security, and love that we thought it would, that we somehow thought was promised to us?

It is into this world the elders must go to serve. They come to this ministry as products of a "world of want in the midst of plenty." They must now also enter the world as God's response. Their mission is to bring about communities of joy in which God is the core and the center.

Look more closely at the state of this mission as it was outlined by the First Presidency's theological statement related to mission:

> Our mission lies in expressing powerful discipleship and in communicating the expectation of spiritual maturity and divine promise to all persons. Aware of the pain and woundedness of all persons, we respond by expressing unconditional love for all and seek for them a faithful relationship with God.[1]

How do elders relate this to the living of their lives of service?

Powerful Discipleship

The elder is called to be a powerful disciple. This does not require great specialization, nor prolonged training, but it does require commitment— a real commitment not only to the *person* of Jesus Christ, but also to the *message* of the Lord Jesus.

Usually people of great personal worth or interest, like today's entertainers or sports figures or even great teachers, find they have disciples. In the main, these individuals are sometimes called "groupies," who simply like to be in the presence of powerful people. Some feel joy, or some sort of recognition, from the presence of a leader.

Often important people also have followers who are not groupies, but rather who agree with or like to be considered in the same light as those they follow. They speak their language and get from the relationship some sort of identity, or self-aggrandizement.

But the Lord calls people not to be groupies, nor scholars and recorders of divine beliefs, but rather to live lives of commitment. Several years ago, as the leaders of the RLDS movement were considering the nature of the church, the First Presidency wrote: "The church of the future will be formed by the living spirit of the One who gathered around him a dozen plain men and shared with them what it is like to live one's life in community."[2] In the simplest of terms, the disciples' calling was to live their lives as God's people within the community; that is, to be disciples of the One who gave them new life.

Disciples are called not just to be witnesses of God's message or recorders of divine words, nor even to bear testimony of magnificent deeds, but to be living examples of a godly life. Central to the calling of the elder is to act out this mission, to be the powerful disciples who live out lives that reflect Christ, to be the expression of the love of the Lord Jesus.

Communicating Spiritual Maturity

The elder is called on to communicate a sense of spiritual maturity. Such an obligation assumes, of course, that the elder involved has achieved some level of personal maturity. It does not mean an elder has arrived at a state of perfection, but rather has moved beyond childish understandings, to see the Creator in terms of his or her own journey.

This elusive maturity is not a point at which elders have arrived, but rather it rests at the end of the journey, calling them forward to even greater and fuller understanding. Those to whom elders offer ministry have a right to know that the elders are pursuing this journey toward maturity, and that while they have not necessarily found all the answers they sought, they have come to love the journey itself.

Communicating such maturity will probably not happen in sermons or meetings, though there is no reason it could not. More likely it will be communicated through the nonjudgmental nature of the woman or man who learns to accept another's beliefs as that person's way of approaching God. Expression of maturity is not in trying to change those beliefs, but in affirming the value of the search, acknowledging the significance of the response, and encouraging an even greater love of God that will, we can assume, lead to an even greater journey of inquiry. That is, we can continue to love that which we know as we seek for better approaches to God.

The Divine Purpose in All People

If the mission of the elder is to bring people to Christ, then our role as disciples may well include the recognition of human nature and the spark of the Creator's desires within people.

The divine purpose is found in Jesus Christ, the model and representative: representative in the sense that it was Christ who introduced us to the loving nature of God and who reflected the power of purpose and the hope of grace. It was the Lord, also, who modeled for us what it means to be a moral person.

It would be difficult to spell out the many aspects of divine purpose, and that is not the intention here. Rather it is to remind elders that the nature of their mission is to represent and model in the same manner as did Christ. Elders are called to be people of worth, to share pain with brothers and sisters, and to be open to the peaceful call of God, who would gather and bless us in our communities.

Aware of the Pain

All people are involved in pain to a degree—if not the pain of being alive and living in imperfect bodies, then the pains of need, loneliness, unbalanced relationships: pains of the heart and soul. Being human often hurts and, to an even larger degree, being a human being involved with others increases the opportunity to be hurt. Certainly we should not be controlled by this pain, or even by the possibility of it. It makes no sense to avoid loving for fear that one might be hurt by love; yet so many people find themselves in this situation.

The call to mission is to not be unaware of the pain of others—a pain that can most often be acknowledged and appreciated because of our own knowledge of pain. For some, this pain is the source of the inquiry; it is the spark of belief.

> Some say that it is a thrill to live these days—that we are filled with a great challenge that calls us with enthusiasm to build a better world. For me it is not that way. Build a better world we shall, but no spirit of enthusiasm calls me. It is not a great challenge that beckons me.

Rather there is a gut hurt that drives me into the world. A vision that begins inside. I see people sick, I see them in pain, I see them alone. The heritage of my children is a world of misery, of selfishness, of hatred and of exploitation. Persons are tired and they are old. No star guides them to a saviour's manger. They desire something better. They are in need. So I search for a better world. The suffering Jesus speaks to me and calls me to share the wounds. And I am thankful for the gut ache that makes my simple world uncomfortable; thankful for the pain that brings me into the lives of others; thankful for the love of those willingly sharing another's pain.[3]

Sometimes it is not the glory of the sunrise that calls us into service. Sometimes it is the dark of sunset. But in either case, it is the call to service.

Respond with Unconditional Love

The promise from our creator is that we are loved. The Creator loves us not because of who we are, but because of who God is. This is the key. It is the moment of understanding about the kind of love God provides and the kind of love we understand God wants from us.

This is not the time to get involved in questions about the kinds and degrees of love. Nor is it about any obligations we have to love because of God's love for us. That is not the point. But there are different expectations of love. One author has suggested that friendship is contrary to Christianity, because friendship means identifying one person we love above all others. Others have suggested that those who would be true servants should not marry. Marriage separates individuals from the rest of the congregation, they suggest, because by loving one person in particular you love the rest less.

Some suggest the only real love open to the clergy is in marrying God or the church itself, for it is the "body of Christ" not the individual that must be loved. But I disagree. I do not think God is asking us to love everyone the same, and thus to acknowledge that we love no one particularly. In fact it is God who uses the particular love of one for another (God for Jesus Christ) to teach us about loving all people.

The key lies in the fact that God loves us. Why does God love us, we ask? We are aware that we are not always lovable. But God loves us because God is a loving God. Out of this essential nature of a loving God, we are loved.

Thus, it seems only reasonable that the call to follow God's commandments to love all people is a call to be a loving person. The question is not whether a person is lovable, or whether or not I wish to love them. Rather it is a fact that because of the essential nature that I love, then I can do nothing else and still be myself.

68

Seek a Faithful Relationship with God

Perhaps the easiest, and the most difficult, of all that has been suggested here is the need to keep a faithful relationship with God. The easy part is because God seeks this relationship and will do more than we expect to help us in this endeavor. The most difficult part is because humans find it hard to maintain relationships, even with God.

Part of the difficulty arises from the fact that few people appear to have a strong relationship with God. Even for those to whom the relationship is paramount, it is difficult to maintain it faithfully. People are inclined to represent themselves and their beliefs differently than they are in practice. Not only is it difficult for all of us to practice what we preach, but often it is hard for us to believe what we think others should believe.

What happens is that in human relationships, people communicate information, even hopes, but rarely convictions. It might be illustrated by looking at the vast amounts of data now being processed electronically that, despite conveying information, omits the sensory experience: the intuitions, the feelings, the contexts of human judgments. It is information without knowledge.

It is the same problem when people seek to relate their faith in God through theological and historical explanations about God. The God so represented reflects what they have discovered is possible, maybe even what they want God to be, but it is not an account of their experience with God. This is not any disfavor for theology or history, rather the realization that talking about one's relationship with God is vastly different from sharing a faithful relationship with God.

Elders are called to provide meaning to the lives of those overwhelmed with material blessings. They must seek out those who only have information and provide them wisdom to give them knowledge. They must find in the love of God, their mission.

> O Amazing God, you come into our ordinary lives
>   and set a holy table among us,
> filling our plates with the Bread of Life
>   and our cups with Salvation.
> Send us out, O God,
>   with tenderheartedness
> to touch an ordinary everyday world
>   with the promise of your holiness.[4]
> > —Ann Weems

Notes

1. Leonard M. Young, *Communities of Joy: New Experiences in Congregational Living* (Independence, Missouri: Herald House, 1994), 70.
2. First Presidency, "The Nature of the Church," handout provided to pastors and in possession of the author, page 1.
3. From a talk delivered by Paul M. Edwards to College Student Conference in Atlanta, Georgia (1979), copy in possession of the author.
4. Ann Weems, "The Ordinary," *Searching for Shalom* (Louisville, Kentucky: Westminster/John Knox Press, 1991), 81. Copyright 1991, Ann Weems. Used by permission of Westminster John Knox Press. All rights reserved.

Chapter 8

Elders as Leaders of Celebration

Ruth Ann Wood

"This is the day which the Lord hath made;
...rejoice and be glad in it."
—Psalm 118:24

Too often people look to their congregational leaders only in times of trauma or discouragement: illness, death, family dissolution. People seem to gravitate toward the church in their moments of crisis, pain, and confusion. They look to elders to provide solace, comfort, and "the peace that passes understanding." Naturally, the church and its leaders are willing to assist at such times, but it is important to remember that the church, too, can share in the joys of human life.

Jesus at the Wedding Feast

At the urging of his mother, Jesus performed his first miracle during the wedding at Cana. Try to imagine the joy and excitement of the wedding guests as they shared together in the creation of a new family in their midst. Imagine music and dancing and the pure joy of community. As the wedding party and the guests celebrated together, there must have been a few—maybe the mother of the bride or the father of the groom—who noticed that the wine supply was low. Try to picture their consternation. What would the guests think? What would the neighbors say about their hospitality? What would happen to the celebration if the refreshments ran out?

In the midst of these concerns, Jesus addressed their need: not the need to alleviate pain and suffering, but the need to celebrate together as a community. In celebration, people gather and share the joy of the successes of life. It is vital to the life and health of individuals and to the families and communities with whom they share their lives to come together and celebrate. Through such celebration together, each life is affirmed, strengthened, and rejoiced.

Meaning and hope are affirmed in congregational celebrations. As individuals share their joys with others, the truth of each one's interrelatedness to others is reaffirmed. Such celebrations remind us that we are a community of friends: each one's victory is my victory; each one's joy fills my heart. Through celebration, congregations acknowledge God's gifts to each one and look to the future as a continuous unfolding of God's blessings.

Stimulation or Elation?

Sometimes in our fast-paced world we mistake stimulation for elation. Stimulation of the senses through loud noises, strong scents, or frantic movement is not necessarily an indication of elation. True joy may result from a deep inner journey based on meditation and complete silence. Elation is the joy that comes from our deepest recesses as we center ourselves in God's love. The frantic search for "thrills" may be a substitute for such deep personal introspection. Many people are so busy "doing things" that they forget to "enjoy life."

Joy is not an end result; the journey is our joy. Each human life is filled with miracles as well as disappointments. It is the work of the church to share with people in all their human experiences. Too often we are afraid to share the "good news" of our lives for fear of alienating those who suffer great sadness. One family in our congregation wanted to postpone their baby's blessing because another family had been separated from their toddler who was hospitalized for an extended period of time. However, after much prayer and consultation with both families, the presiding elder encouraged the family to schedule their baby's blessing as a positive symbol of support for all children in our congregation whether they were physically present or not. It is in the commingling of joy and sadness that we share with one another who we truly are and find acceptance.

Barbara Howard[1] shares a wonderful story of the celebration of the life of her mother-in-law, Audrey Howard. Despite the pain of losing her, the family wanted to share the joy of her life as they planned her memorial service: they asked friends to share stories of the joy of knowing Audrey; her grandchildren shared wonderful memories. The service included her favorite music, a table of memorabilia, and photographs of a wonderful, full life of love and happiness.

Acknowledging the Indwelling Spirit

Celebration is the act of acknowledging the power of God's indwelling Spirit. As we look inside ourselves, we find a complexity of emotions. Some of us have survived intense trauma, and our joys have been forged on the anvil of great personal pain. Others have lived well-paced and placid lives, whose joys reflect satisfaction with life's stability. Barbara Howard wrote, "The journey of joy is more than laughing together.... It is a willingness to share pain and struggle."[2] Too many people put on a "Sunday face" when they go into church. This "Sunday face" is a shield— it protects them from clearly seeing others as well as preventing others from seeing them as vulnerable and in need of ministry. Such masks prevent us from reading the true story of their struggles. People try to hide their true selves and keep others at a distance—they don't want to bother anybody. But shouldn't our congregations be the safest places to reveal the true patterns of our lives?

Celebration as an Act of Compassion

As we come together in community, we learn to address each other with compassion. Compassion is the emotion that allows us to share each other's suffering as a joyful opportunity to lighten another's load. The hymn (*HS* 369) reminds us: "Divine love revealing, Wherever we meet human need." A young man in our congregation suffers from a chronic illness and, at first, tried to mask his pain and despair. However, as people shared their own pain and struggles with him, he began to feel comfortable letting his mask slip occasionally. When his sharing was met with compassion and empathy rather than home remedies and harangues about repentance, he felt safe. Over time, he has shared openly about the extent of his pain and hopelessness. The physical realities of his illness have changed little in the last few years, but his joy in being a part of our community has been a life-enriching experience for him and for our congregation.

Celebration—A Way of Life

Henri Nouwen, a Dutch theologian who died in 1996, explained that celebration should be a way of life:

> Celebration is not just a way to make people feel good for a while; it is the way in which faith in the God of life is lived out, through both laughter and tears. Thus celebration goes beyond ritual, custom, and tradition. It is the unceasing affirmation that underneath all the ups and downs of life there flows a solid current of

joy.... Joy offers the solid ground from which new life can always burst. Joy can be caught neither in one feeling or emotion nor in one ritual or custom but is always more than we expect, always surprising, and therefore always a sign that we are in the presence of the Lord of life.[3]

When our daughter, Melanie, was baptized, the presider asked her to choose her favorite hymn for the congregation to sing as they awaited her return after her baptism. Her immediate and enthusiastic response was, "Joy to the World!" The presider looked slightly confused (after all, Christmas hymns are not often sung in July). However, when he announced to the congregation that Melanie had chosen this special hymn, the voices rang out with great enthusiasm and joy. The celebration of her baptism was one filled with the hope and promise of this young child who had been nurtured and loved in this community.

The Celebration of Congregational Life

Leonard Young in *Communities of Joy*[4] offered six expressions of celebration for the congregation:

1. *The Joy of Family.* The family dimension of congregational life gives each person the feeling of being loved as brother, sister, parent, and child. Families have successes and failures, joys and sorrows. Families are healthy and often unhealthy. To be the "family of God" a congregation is called to exemplify the best of family life. When we discover that we are loved regardless of our problems, quirks, and disfunctionalities, it is at this point that we experience the spirit of the congregation as family. In the congregational family, caring is expressed through remembering birthdays, celebrating new children, rejoicing at weddings, grieving with the bereaved, applauding the achiever, and standing with the struggling. The church living in the image of a family is a primary way to express celebration in the congregation.

2. *The Joy of Fellowship.* The church that meets and eats together stays together. That may sound like a simple statement, but it has profound implications. The bond between members of a congregation is strengthened in moments of intimate interrelating. There are few things more intimate and self-revealing than sitting down for a meal with others. Congregations that have a strong tradition of potluck dinners, family nights, congregational birthday parties, and social groups have a strong sense of the joy of fellowship. When the Saints look forward to being together for activities and events that are not directly related to worship on Sunday morning, the spirit of fellowship is being expressed. The ministry of fellowship is the

grease that lubricates the rough spots and allows a congregation to work together. When we spend time with others, we learn who they are and they learn who we are. In this way, we become bonded to each other as our fellowship increases.

3. *The Joy of Being Cared For.* In moments of deep need, the touch of another's hand or a word of concern can turn life around. The church celebrates the importance and worth of every individual when each one is cared for with love and compassion. In congregations where the spirit of caring is central, people find Christ in the lives of others and let the Christ within them minister to others. Caring is an essential part of congregational celebration. When caring is present the congregation is a warm place where everyone wants to be.

4. *The Joy of Learning.* In families there is a strong desire to help children grow to become all that they are capable of becoming. Families often sacrifice heavily to send children through school. Many times parents put off doing things they would like to do just so their children can have opportunities to learn that they never had. The church is committed to learning for all of God's children in the same way. Congregations that place a high priority on expressing the joy of learning will focus intentionally on Christian education, Temple School, and other important educational opportunities. Celebrating each other suggests that we offer everyone the opportunity to learn and grow in God's image. The joy of learning is a central part of congregational celebration.

5. *The Joy of Worshiping God.* Worship is a central act to Christian life. When disciples meet together to pray, sing, testify, read scripture, and listen to the word, they are celebrating the body of Christ. Some of the most profound moments of joy in my life have come as I have joined with other Christians in moments of praise and prayer. Worship as a form of celebration is positive, uplifting, Christ-centered, and focused on ministering to human hurts, hopes, and needs. Christians must have a dynamic worship life if the spirit of celebration is to live among them. Congregational health and vitality are often related to the spirit of joy found in the celebration of the Saints through worship.

6. *The Joy of Giftedness.* In order to celebrate life as a gift from God, it is necessary to see human beings as creations endowed with great potential and many gifts by their creator. The process of identifying and freeing the gifts of every person for ministry is another way to express joy through congregational life. If our congregations

are places that foster creativity, inquiry, experimentation, learning, and growth, individual disciples will discover their gifts from God and apply them to ministry. In this way the congregation will progressively expand its capability to offer ministry to its members and to its community. The awareness of personal giftedness and a commitment to utilize these gifts in ministry is a fundamental part of the celebration dimension of congregational life.

Why wait to celebrate?

Paul Pearsall, in his book *Super Joy*, says, "If we wait for everything we want accomplished to be completed before we celebrate, we will miss the party of life."[5] How often does our community wait for a milestone before it celebrates its members? Christmas? weddings? graduation? new babies? What would your community feel like if it also celebrated a fish caught by a six year old or a new hip for an eighty year old? Where are the points of joy in the life of your congregation that could be celebrated? Where are the occasions of pure joy that, too often, we keep to ourselves? What would our community be like if we intentionally celebrated the ordinariness of our life together?

To You!

by Ann Weems[6]

This morning I was toasted by a two year old
Who raised her orange juice glass to mine and said, "To you!"
She brought the morning; she moved a mountain;
She brought flowers out of barren land and sunlight from darkness.
What a way to start the day—affirmed and celebrated!

Remember to celebrate those across the breakfast table.
When did you last tell them they are precious?
You told them to take out the trash, to make their beds,
But did you tell them they are cherished?

You told them they were wrong; you told them to hurry up;
But did you tell them they are beautiful?
We celebrate events or days or heroes,
But take for granted the joy of the familiar.

76

So here's to you, familiar faces at my breakfast table!
Here's to smiles, sleepy kisses, and theological questions at dawn!
Here's to unbrushed teeth, unmade beds, and unpicked-up clothes!
Here's to dirty tennis shoes with one blue sock and one brown!
Here's to last night's scores and news told before I read it!
Here's to my cold cup of coffee, to the lunch forgotten!
Here's to the little girl who wants ice cream with her eggs!
Here's to the daddy who thinks that's funny!
Here's to the man who loves us so and lets us know!
I cherish you who breakfast with me.
You are sun in my rain—sustenance and star.

O Lord, free us to thank God for each other!
Free us to click orange juice glasses clear across your Kingdom.
In every family and in the larger family of the gathered church.
Here's to you, saints who remembered to love!
Here's to those who heal, teach, listen, comfort;
Who feed the hungry, clothe the naked, give a cup of cold water,
Weep with those who weep, rejoice with those who rejoice,
And stand by to pick us up and brush us off!
Here's to the peacemakers and the prophets—
Their justice, their mercy, their humility,

Their strength that does not falter!
Here's to those who have been freed to free us,
To their song that never ends,
To the saints who keep on dancing!
Here's to you!

Notes

1.   Barbara Howard, *Journey of Joy* (Independence, Missouri: Herald House, 1990), 79.
2.   Ibid., 11.
3.   Henri Nouwen, *Lifesigns: Intimacy, Fecundity, and Ecstasy in Christian Perspective* (Garden City, New York: Doubleday, 1986), 102.
4.   Leonard Young, *Communities of Joy: New Experiences in Congregational Living* (Independence, Missouri: Herald House, 1994), 97–99.
5.   Paul Pearsall, *Super Joy: In Love with Living* (New York: Bantam Books, 1988), 60.
6.   Ann Weems, *Reaching for Rainbows: Resources for Creative Worship* (Philadelphia: Westminster Press, 1980), 31. Copyright 1980, Ann Weems. Used by permission of Westminster John Knox Press. All rights reserved.

Chapter 9

The Elder's Commitment to Joy

Jeanne Earnest

We appear to know very little about joy even though scriptural references to "joy" abound. It's unfortunate to have to acknowledge this lack of understanding because it implies that we Christians are not really doing our jobs. As Samuel M. Shoemaker put it, "The surest mark of a Christian is not faith, or even love, but joy."[1] Where is our joy? Is it readily available, and we are simply overlooking it? Is it strictly God-given and, therefore, not within our power to generate? Is it so fleeting, elusive, and temporary that seeking it is pure folly? Where does joy exist? Is it possible to sustain?

For elders, these are important and necessary questions. Because we are told "[People] are, that they might have joy" (II Nephi 1:115), we can only conclude that it is utmost in God's scheme of things that all of humankind experience "joy." That being the case, it would be easy to justify the idea that elders need to be about the business of encouraging and emphasizing joyful living. How is that done exactly? It probably must occur on at least two levels. First, we can't teach others to know joy if we ourselves have not known it. Second, if we find joy attainable and discover it firsthand, then we must most certainly set about learning how to introduce it into the lives of others. Surely joy is to be shared and magnified with those we love.

But what exactly constitutes joy? That is a difficult question to answer. Perhaps it can only be answered by individuals who seek to know. Certainly the scriptures give us plenty of signposts for our journey toward joy. We are told, for example, in Galatians 5:22 that, "...the fruit of the Spirit is love, joy, peace..." In other words, what grows from Spirit, what blossoms and develops from spirituality includes joy. It could be postulated then that spiritual cultivation results in joy. That being true, it follows that joy might be had by pursuing actively a close personal relationship with God. But how?

Spiritual disciplines have been delineated since people first sought God: prayer, meditation, fasting, study, service, as well as submission, solitude, simplicity, confession, and worship. But these disciplines need to be enlivened by a passionate sense of expectation and longing. Can we even imagine what it would be like to walk and talk with God on a daily or even hourly basis? Do we imagine ourselves hiding from God in shame much like Adam and Eve? Have we come to view ourselves as unworthy partakers of such an intimate association and, therefore, expend little energy even in the anticipation of such a union? Have our religious institutions been better at teaching us to feel guilty rather than to feel and expect joy?

In the Jewish tradition, David, the shepherd boy, is believed by many to be the most beloved son of God. This comes as no surprise when the Psalms give witness to the intensity and passion that undergirded David's relationship to God in heaven. His writings reveal such joyous hope and passionate devotion to his personal God that they nearly sing out in their praise for God: "Then will I go unto the altar of God, unto God my exceeding joy; yea, upon the harp will I praise thee, O God my God" (Psalm 43:4). And in Psalm 119:10 we find: "With my whole heart have I sought thee; O let me not wander from thy commandments." In verse 40, "Behold, I have longed after thy precepts; quicken me in thy righteousness." In his words we find all the elements of passion, praise, longing, trust, expectation, dependence, devotion, and joy.

As we read David's psalms we can't help but be moved by the total surrender of his willfulness and his strong desire to become a faithful servant: "O how I love thy law! it is my meditation all the day" (Psalm 119:97). What qualities are inherent in this young man that predisposed him to such a fervent search for his creator? Did he know solitude, simplicity, discipline, prayer? Where does his passion and longing for connection come from? Surely his attitude contributed greatly to God being able to use him for the accomplishment of divine purposes on numerous occasions. Notice again, however, that God was able to utilize David for God's work even though David fell far short of perfection.

It seems clear that God doesn't require perfect obedience as much as God requires passionate desire. Augustine advises: "If you would never cease to pray, never cease to long for it. The continuance of your longing is the continuance of your prayer." Do we seek our Master with such urgency and ardor? Do we expect from God the same measure of passion and intensity? If not, why not? We are God's treasures. We are

God's joy. The story of the Prodigal (Luke 15:20–24) dramatically illustrates our eternal value and tells us in no uncertain terms how joyful the father was:

> And he arose and came to his father. But when he was yet a great way off, his father saw him, and had compassion, and ran, and fell on his neck, and kissed him. And the son said unto him, Father, I have sinned against heaven, and in thy sight, and am no more worthy to be called thy son. But the father said unto his servants, Bring forth the best robe, and put it on him; and put a ring on his finger, and shoes on his feet; And bring hither the fatted calf, and kill it; and let us eat and be merry; For this my son was dead, and is alive again; he was lost, and is found. And they began to be merry.

We matter a great deal to God. If we understood and believed in our own worth, we would see that God would respond to us in kind. God awaits our decision to make our way back to the Divine and will rush out to greet us and embrace us while we are still a great way off. We have within us not only the power to experience great joy ourselves but to actually create joy through the One who loves us beyond all reason.

What keeps us from such a reunion with God? Partly it's our attitudes that render us ineffectual. In our present lives of abundance with so many choices to make, we are nearly drowning in a sea of options. Too many choices, too many decisions, and too many opportunities to pass up leave us feeling overwhelmed and overburdened. Our lives get swallowed up by the ever-present awareness that there is so much out there for the taking.

Our attitude has become one of needing to "fill ourselves up." But we don't know how to fill up our hearts and our souls—just our bodies and our minds. We can fill up our bodies with food and sensual pleasures galore, and we can fill up our minds with television and movies and computer games, but how do you fill up a soul and feed a hungry spirit? The paradox is that we can fill up the soul by finding the empty spaces and entering into them. That's where we will find God. That's why meditation, prayer, solitude, fasting, and focused breathing can lead us to the Divine.

God is to be found in the stillness, in the vast void that is filled to the brim with potential. We live in a time when it is hard to be still and know God. We are bombarded and tempted on all sides by busyness, noise, time constraints, deadlines, telephones, faxes, billboards, pagers, and electronic mail messages—everything clamors for our attention. We are paying less and less attention in the midst of the dizzying array. But it's difficult to tune it all out and pull back to ourselves, let alone to God. In Marianne Williamson's book, *Illuminata*, she writes:

We try to consume the external, to give us a feeling of internal satisfaction. And yet we cannot satisfy that yearning, because nothing outside of us is the stuff for which we hunger. The more we grab, the less centered we are. And so we disintegrate; we do not grow. We take on the characteristics of neurotic, needy people, for that is who we decide to be when we look to the world for what the world cannot give us.

It is imperative, therefore, that we give time each day, each week, to silence, to the internal search, to honoring God before the world.

We must embrace the void instead of resisting it. That is the way of the mystic. It is the only way we can heal.[2]

Human beings are, in the final analysis, spiritual creatures. Our fundamental nature is spiritual and eternal. Deepak Chopra, physician and author of *Ageless Body, Timeless Mind*, teaches us that although each person seems separate and independent, all of us are connected to patterns of intelligence that govern the whole cosmos. Our bodies are part of a universal body, our minds an aspect of a universal mind. We now know that every atom in the universe is 99.999 percent empty space, and subatomic particles move at lightning speed through this space carrying information and vibrating energy. In fact, "The three-dimensional body reported by the five senses is a mirage."[3]

Everyone has a prejudice in favor of things that are reassuringly three-dimensional, as reported to us by our five senses. Sight, hearing, touch, taste, and smell serve to reinforce the same message: things are what they seem. According to this reality, the Earth is flat, the ground beneath your feet is stationary, the sun rises in the east and sets in the west, all because it seems that way to the senses. As long as the five senses were accepted without question, such facts were immutable.

Einstein realized that time and space are also products of our five senses; we see and touch things that occupy three dimensions, and we experience events as happening in sequential order. Yet Einstein and his colleagues were able to remove this mask of appearances. They reassembled time and space into a new geometry that had no beginning or end, no edges, no solidity. Every solid particle in the universe turned out to be a ghostly bundle of energy vibrating in an immense void.

The old space-time model was smashed, replaced by a timeless, flowing field of constant transformation. This quantum field isn't separate from us—it *is* us. Where Nature goes to create stars, galaxies, quarks, and leptons, you and I go to create ourselves. The great advantage of this new worldview is that it is so immensely creative—the human body, like everything else in the cosmos, is constantly being made anew every second. Although your senses report that you inhabit a solid body in time and space, this is only the most superficial layer of reality. Your body is something far more miraculous—a flowing organism empowered by millions of years of intelligence. This intelligence is dedicated to overseeing the constant change that takes place inside you. Every cell is a miniature terminal connected to the cosmic computer.[4]

Our ability to maintain awareness is who we really are. "Deep inside us, unknown to the five senses, is an innermost core of being, a field of non-change that creates personality.... This seer is the spirit, the expression of eternal being."[5] We are, in fact, reflections, fragments, expressions, representations, if you will, of the Divine. It appears we are each separate from one another and from God but, in fact, we are all elements of an ever-changing, continuous stream of awareness, intelligence, and wholeness linked inextricably to all of the universe and its parts. To find what we need, we must go deep inside ourselves and search out the empty spaces to find God, ourselves, and ultimately, joy. When we discover our true value and our true selves, we will experience the "awe" of the miracle and the meaning of our lives. Joy will become an attitude, a way of perceiving that permeates all our thoughts. Joy will not be tied to circumstances the way happiness is. Joy will be the result of coming into harmony with God's will and purpose. It is not a state that necessarily comes into being when we "will" it. It is often the culmination of living and practicing the spiritual disciplines. Other times, joy comes as a gift, serendipitously bestowed. All we can do is prepare to receive it and expect its imminent arrival.

With this gift of joy comes a transformation of the spirit. When we walk and talk with God, we can truly experience not just joy but the other fruits of the Spirit as well. The transformation creates within us a profound change where we align ourselves with things eternal rather than finite. We can cease to worry; we can let go of our fears and concerns and experience a deepening sense of trust, assurance, and dependency on a personal God who is actively present and involved in our lives. Too much to ask for? Too good to be true? Too unrealistic for our times? How are we any different from the biblical figures who walked and talked with God? Of course, it is available to each of us, and we are commissioned as elders to assist others in attaining the joy of a close personal relationship with God that was always meant for us to have.

In Nehemiah 8:10 we read, "...the joy of the Lord is your strength." Joy is something we can make a commitment to and choose to embrace—it's not something that we must sit and wait to befall us. People tend to postpone joy while waiting for their circumstances to justify its presence. It's as if we think of joy as something that comes to us in the form of something wonderful happening to us and causing us to feel great joy. In point of fact, we can choose joy, expect joy, and be strengthened by joy no matter what our circumstances are.

> Though the fig tree does not blossom, and no fruit is on the vines; though the produce of the olive fails and the fields yield no food; though the flock is cut off from the fold and there is no herd in the stalls, yet I will rejoice in the Lord; I will ex-

ult in the God of my salvation. God, the Lord is my strength; [God] makes my feet like the feet of a deer, and makes me tread upon the heights.

—Habakkuk 3:17–19 NRSV

Our perceptions are everything. How we think about things predisposes us to our reactions. Albert Ellis, a well-known psychologist, informs us that events do not cause emotional reactions. Rather how we view or perceive these events causes the accompanying emotional responses. When a person is being mugged, the event of a police officer arriving at the scene creates panic in the mugger but relief in the victim. The event itself must be interpreted by the individual and given meaning. Therefore, we are called on to see God's hand at work in all things, which then allows us to infuse events with our own meanings—even to the point that we can find meaning in our sufferings and tribulations.

Beloved, think it not strange concerning the fiery trial which is to try you, as though some strange thing happened unto you; But rejoice, inasmuch as ye are partakers of Christ's sufferings; that when his glory shall be revealed, ye may be glad also with exceeding joy.—I Peter 4:12–13

We are called to rejoice ever more, to pray unceasingly, and in everything give thanks (see I Thessalonians 5:16–18). This is God's will and it resonates within each of us. Lewis Smedes wrote,

You and I were created for joy, and if we miss it, we miss the reason for our existence!...If our joy is honest joy, it must somehow be congruous with human tragedy. This is the test of joy's integrity: is it compatible with pain?...Only the heart that hurts has a right to joy.[6]

Again we encounter one of the paradoxes of life—that the more sorrow we bear, the greater our capacity is for joy—as if sorrow carves out a hollow place in our soul that joy can then potentially fill up.

So if, as elders, we seek to establish within ourselves an attitude of joyfulness even in the midst of tears, how can this benefit others? Certainly joy is not a single, unilateral kind of effect. It is not a constant or something easily measured or even identified. The blissful, ecstatic joy of falling in love or becoming a new parent differs in kind from the quiet, contented joy of a lifelong friendship or tranquil looking back at the cherished moments of a lifetime.

But what is the nature of joy that can strengthen us spiritually over time and provide solace to those in despair? We know there is much misery and tragedy in the world. What keeps us faithful in our commitment to joy? The answer is found in Galatians 2 with the reminder that God loves and cherishes *who we are*, not *what we do* for God. The Creator does not need us to *do* anything. God calls us to be somebody for the Divine Purpose. None of us can become perfect by keeping the rules and working hard to please God. It's already been done. Christ was the perfect One. And now, because of that obedience to God's will, we are invited through God's grace and Christ's sacrifice, to enter into a loving, intimate relationship with our creator. Eugene Peterson wrote:

> If a living relationship with God came by rule keeping, then Christ died gratuitously. We are justified by faith in Christ. Justification means being put together the way we are supposed to be. Made right—not improved, not decorated, not veneered, not patched up, but justified. Our fundamental being is set in right relationship with God. This setting right is not impersonal fixing; it is personal reconciliation. We are never right in ourselves, but only in response to and as a result of God working in and through us.[7]

Now there is a reason to feel joy. We were lost and have been found—all our sins forgiven and we are greeted by an adoring Parent who runs to us and embraces us though we have done nothing to deserve such love except to belong to God.

We must learn as well to appreciate and savor many of the easily "taken for granted" gifts from God if we are to maintain our sense of joy. The very miracle of our lives—the fact that we are and have the grace of everyday living along with opportunities to stand in God's stead in the world—is an awesome reality. Do not regret growing older. It is a privilege denied to many. Life is indeed sacred. "Just to be is a blessing. Just to live is holy," wrote Abraham Heschel.

We need to remind each other to live expectantly—believing that God is relentless in the divine quest to make God known to each of us. In fact, it is quite possible that God needs to receive our love in order to have fullness of divine love.

Sometimes it's worth remembering that it is a gospel of "good news" that we send out. So often we become weighed down and burdened by the seriousness of our "church work" that we forget to be glad. We forget that we have been redeemed and saved, and we can actually expect "goodness and mercy to follow us all the days of our lives and we shall dwell in the house of the Lord forever" (adapted Psalm 23:6).

How do we lose sight of such "good news"? Do we live in a state of high expectancy anticipating regular encounters with the Divine? Or do we see ourselves as more or less running things on our own? Is it lack of self-esteem that hinders our expectations? In our desire to be humble, meek, and avoid the appearance of haughtiness or arrogance, we may overstep the line and create attitudes of inadequacies, worthlessness, and devaluation instead of quiet confidence and a strong sense of self.

In the not-too-distant past, church school teachers devised what they felt was a perfect way to depict the concept of true joy to their young charges. They used the word "joy" as an acronym and taught them that the way to ensure everlasting joy was to remember what the letters themselves could stand for: J=Jesus, O=others, and Y=you with a strong emphasis on the order being important. If one remembered to always put Jesus first, others second, and you last in life, then this would lead to the ultimate secret formula for lasting joy.

Unfortunately, this approach tended to be a great formula for codependency, resentment, guilt-in-making, and self-defeating behaviors as well. The formula failed to include the importance of individual emotional needs which, if left unmet, resulted in feelings of hollowness, frustration, depression, and anger. Denial of self doesn't necessarily lead one directly to joy.

Of course, a basic tenet of many religions is the idea that people are called to be concerned with the welfare and needs of others and not just focused on selfish interests. But the question that looms is, are we acting selfishly when we attend to our own personal needs? Or are we in fact acting responsibly by assuming that it is up to us to ensure that our needs are met and we are filled? From such a state of abundance, we then truly do have something to give away. That is to say, that we serve most lovingly and willingly when our own cup runneth over than if we try to keep reaching down deep into an empty well to quench the thirst of others when we don't even know how to quench our own parched throats.

With Jesus as our example, do we see him as a person of deprivation, self-abasement, and masochism who continually gave until spent? Is this the important message of the cross? Is sacrifice to the point of martyrdom the call for all good Christians? Are each of us called to this measure of sacrificial living at all times? Or is there also a call for us to live lives of abundance now that the ultimate sacrifice has been made for us?

Does God require abstinence and deprivation at all times and from all people or did Jesus make for all of us the sacrifice that would set us all free to live lives of joyful abundance and generosity? Do I help others better by means of extreme asceticism and the wearing of sackcloth to signify my devout dedication to suffering, or might I be called to a life of celebration and commitment to joy because my Redeemer lives? Do I glorify Jesus' death or do I glorify his gift of life to me and live it to the fullest possible measure and never forget that to whom much is given much is required? Out of the abundance can come chosen responses of love, obedience, service, and generous offerings even to the point of sacrifice if need be.

Of course, the issue is not so simplistically "either/or." Certainly there is a time for joy and indeed time for sorrow. It just appears that the world cries out for people who can demonstrate that faith does in fact lead to joy and not just to a monkish existence of serious contemplation and a sense of indebtedness.

Let us consider the notion that what God may truly desire for people is, in fact, joy. In Deuteronomy 30:19 we find these words: "...I have set before you life and death, blessing and cursing: therefore choose life, that both thou and thy seed may live." And we are admonished that:

> The elders and [people] of the church should be of cheerful heart and countenance among themselves and in their intercourse with their neighbors and [others] of the world... Let the young...cultivate the gifts of music and of song; let not the middle-aged and the old forget the gladsomeness of their youth and let them aid and assist so far as their cares will permit; and remember that Saints should be cheerful in their warfare that they may be joyous in their triumph...and in cheerfulness do whatever may be permitted you to perform that the blessing of peace may be upon all.—Doctrine and Covenants 119:3a, 6d, 9c

In essence, joy depends on passionate expectation. The elder's responsibility is to restore expectation among the people, and God's joy will emerge as an underlying attitude. What we can reasonably expect is that:

1. God longs to be in relationship with each of us.
2. If we seek God's presence, God will make God known to us.
3. The Creator will respond when we create empty spaces in our lives (via the spiritual disciplines) for God to fill.
4. God will keep divine promises and do more than just hear us and care about us. God will enthusiastically engage us and lift us up to a higher dimension of living, where priorities get shifted and we gain a bigger picture of who we are and how we connect to everything in the entire universe. "The emptiness at the core of every atom is the womb of the universe; in the flicker of thought when two neurons interact there is an opportunity for a new world to be born."[8]

We may desire to bring to the Lord a perfect work. We would like to point, when our work is done, to the beautiful ripened grain and bound-up sheaves, and yet the Lord frustrates our plans, shatters our purposes, lets us see the wreck of all our hopes, breaks the beautiful structure we thought we were building, and catches us up in his arms and whispers to us, "It's not your work I wanted, but you."

In the end, our goal shall be to embrace the attitude conveyed in II Corinthians 6:10: We know sorrow, yet our joy is inextinguishable.

Notes

1. Tim Hansel, *You Gotta Keep Dancin': In the Midst of Life's Hurts, You Can Choose Joy!* (Elgin, Illinois, David C. Cook Publishing, 1985), 51.
2. Marianne Williamson, *Illuminata: Thoughts, Prayers, Rites of Passage* (New York: Random House, 1994), 104–105.
3. Deepak Chopra, *Ageless Body, Timeless Mind: The Quantum Alternative to Growing Old* (New York: Harmony Books, 1993), 44.
4. Ibid., 7–8.
5. Ibid., 7.
6. Lewis B. Smedes, *How Can It Be All Right When Everything Is All Wrong?* (San Francisco: Harper & Row, 1982), 11, 15.
7. Eugene H. Peterson, *Traveling Light: Reflections on the Free Life* (Downers Grove, Illinois: InterVarsity Press, 1982).
8. Chopra, 40.

Epilogue

The Elder and the Great Awakening

Paul M. Edwards

This book has been written in conjunction with the Elders and Congregational Leaders event held in Independence, Missouri, at the RLDS Temple (June 1997). It is designed to encourage and support the elders in their work. But it, like the conference, is primarily concerned with the "going forth" of the work of the elders. For as you leave the gathering of your peers, or as you raise your head from the pages of this book, the proof of your commitment lies in the service of your ministry. It is a calling to mission: to the great awakening of God's people.

In its long and interesting history, the Western world has gone through three "great awakenings." Each lasted about a century and began as a movement of great passion that, in time, resulted in new religious denominations, renewed ethics, enhanced moral concerns, and increased spirituality.

The first of these awakenings was about 1730, and it grew from moral anger. This anger emphasized spiritual rebirth and moral rejuvenation based on the utilitarian model. It was, to a large extent, the ideological source of the American Revolution.

The second, which we time with the turn of the nineteenth century, arose out of the passionate response to human failure and pushed the century before it to a reaffirmation of salvation by grace. This awakening affirmed that the unlimited love of God was the only hope to rise from the fierce struggle against corruption, particularly inner corruption. The degrees of the passion that drove it gave birth to so many of the "single-issue" programs we still face today, like abortion and temperance.

The third of these great awakenings took place about 1890 and resulted, we believe, from the crises of culture and human identification created by urbanization and industrialization, which swept the world unchecked. It provided hope in the social efforts of good people to recreate their society, providing the moral groundwork for science and capitalism. It was the birth mother of welfarism, labor reform, and a return to social gospelism.

The fourth of these awakenings is happening now. It comes to us, as did the others, from the passionate response to a world gone astray. It grows from a rebellion against selfishness (the internal preoccupation of

the "me" generation with the seemingly unrestrained desire for imme-
diacy) and from sexual and moral debauchery, overindulgence, and greed.
The great wish is to replace this movement with family identification, simplistic government, ethical universalism, and growing individual and social responsibility.

So far, much of this new awakening has been brought about by a
growth of mystical experience and direct-link spirituality that brings about
primary changes in the life of an individual.*

Just where the individual elder, or the RLDS Church, fits into this
growing awareness is yet to be determined. But it would be foolish for
us not to realize that it is happening, and that while we might all have
difficulties with the language or descriptions of the followers, they are in
the main good people in search of a meaningful life under their God and
the Lord Jesus Christ.

At the moment, the great lesson they teach us is that of passion. That
is, they reflect a movement of people who believe they have felt the power
of Jesus Christ and are so changed by it that they are willing to direct their
passion to the spreading of the word.

When we consider our roles as elders, let us remember that the people
of the world seek a new awareness, a great awakening. They are spiritually low, they are harassed by the misdirection of their own visions, and
they need to hear the story. The call of elders, in addition to the many
other tasks that consume their energy, talent, and time, is to spread the
word. The word is this: *You must love more; there is no other way.*

---

*These four phases of awakening are inspired by Robert Fogel and have been taken from
personal notes on his Bradley Lecture, given on September 11, 1995, at the American
Enterprise Institute.

Bibliography

Obviously there is not a large reserve of works that address the role of the elder in the Reorganized Church of Jesus Christ of Latter Day Saints. However, there are some, and they are included. In addition, there are a few books that we recommend to help you identify and perform your task. Some are old (possibly out of print) and need to be located in a library or used-book store, but they are worth the trouble. Some can be picked up easily. These are our recommendations:

Bouissou, Jean-Christophe. *Christ and Community*. Independence, Missouri: Herald House, 1996.

Briskin, Alan. *The Stirring of Soul in the Workplace*. San Francisco: Jossey-Bass, 1996.

Church Peacemaker Skills, Temple School Course AM133, 1992.

Davis, Dwight D. W. *The Ministry of the Elder: A Manual for Priesthood Study and Reference*. Independence, Missouri: Herald House, 1953.

Edwards, Paul M., ed. *Aaronic Foundational Ministries*. Independence, Missouri: Herald House, 1996.

The Elder, Temple School Course PA104, 1996.

Fowler, James W. *Weaving the New Creation: Stages of Faith and the Public Church*. San Francisco: HarperSanFrancisco, 1991.

Fromm, Erich. *To Have or To Be?* New York: Harper and Row, 1976.

Keen, Sam. *Hymns to an Unknown God: Awakening the Spirit in Everyday Life*. New York: Bantam Books, 1994.

_____. *The Passionate Life: Stages of Loving*. San Francisco: Harper & Row, 1983.

Judd, Peter A. *Worship in a Diverse Culture*. Independence, Missouri: Herald House, 1995.

Martin, Mike W. *Everyday Morality: An Introduction to Applied Ethics*. Belmont, California: Wadsworth Publishing, 1995.

Ministry and the Physically Ill, Temple School Course AL340, 1996.

Ministry with Persons, Temple School Course CL100, 1991.

Nouwen, Henri J. M. *The Return of the Prodigal Son*. New York: Doubleday, 1992.

Novak, Michael. *Ascent of the Mountain, Flight of the Dove: An Invitation to Religious Studies.* San Francisco: Harper & Row, 1978.

Prince, Gregory A. *Power from on High: The Development of Mormon Priesthood.* Salt Lake City, Utah: Signature Books, 1995.

Public Ministry Foundations, Temple School Course AM141, 1995.

The Role of the Pastor, Temple School Course PA125, 1984.

Sample, Tex. *U.S. Lifestyles and Mainline Churches: A Key to Reaching People in the 90s.* Louisville, Kentucky: Westminister/John Knox Press, 1990.

Sinetar, Marsha. *Ordinary People as Monks and Mystics: Lifestyles for Self-discovery.* New York: Paulist Press, 1986.

Spencer, Geoffrey F. *The Promise of Healing.* Independence, Missouri: Herald House, 1993.

Storr, Anthony. *Solitude: A Return to the Self.* New York: Ballantine Books, 1988.

Tyree, Alan D. *Priesthood: For Others' Sake.* Independence, Missouri: Herald House, 1996.

Weaver, Richard M. *Ideas Have Consequences.* Chicago: University of Chicago Press, 1965.

Young, Leonard M. *Communities of Joy: New Experiences in Congregational Living.* Independence, Missouri: Herald House, 1994.